BUSINESS DECISIONS

BUSINESS DECISIONS

A CROSS-MODULAR CASE STUDY APPROACH

Joseph Chilver
B.Sc.Econ.Hons. (Lond.), A.I.B. (& Trustee Dip.), Dip. C.M.

MACMILLAN

First published 1983
Reprinted 1986

Published by
MACMILLAN EDUCATION LTD
Houndmills, Basingstoke, Hampshire RG21 2XS
and London
Companies and representatives
throughout the world

Printed in Hong Kong

ISBN 0–333–34497–9 (hardcover)
ISBN 0–333–34498–7 (paperback)

Contents

Preface

This book contains a graduated selection of case studies providing material for the training of business executives. Drawing upon a variety of disciplines and study areas, students are invited to solve the problems which have been set for them in a series of realistic scenarios. The problems posed are such as face top-level managers in various firms at one stage of development or another. They present a challenge to any student of business and/or any aspiring manager. Nevertheless, the programme has been designed with specific courses in mind. First, the intention is to provide stimulating material for those on Higher National Level courses of the Business Education Council. The cases provide a framework for an assortment of cross-modular assignments and the appropriate themes of people, finance, communication and problem-solving are substantially incorporated. Another important group catered for are those studying for the Diploma of the Institute of Commercial Management. The subject of business policy in particular requires case analysis coupled with group discussion, and the material here provides an appropriate course of study. The final group in mind are those on business degree courses featuring integrative studies. The battery of cases which follow should contribute something towards the development of the analytic and decision-making skills called for. There are Guidelines in the final section which should help students to understand the sort of approach envisaged.

While the case studies included here model situations frequently encountered in business, the names of characters and companies used in the scenarios are wholly fictional.

JOSEPH CHILVER

Acknowledgements

The author and publishers wish to thank the following for permission to include various extracts as acknowledged in the text:

The Sunday Telegraph
The Guardian
Financial Times
The Observer
The Sunday Times
Trusthouse Forte Plc

The author also wishes to thank Messrs A. F. Somerville Ford and Colman Hanrahan of the Business Studies Centre, Bournemouth, for their contributions.

Introduction

Business can be studied from a variety of angles, though tradition-
ally training has been compartmentalised in such convenient pockets
of study as economics, statistics, accounting and law. Recently
however, the demarcation lines have been under scrutiny and have
been substantially revised, at least on those courses under the
auspices of the Business Education Council. Controversy is
inevitable when changes of such a magnitude are introduced,
particularly in an academic world where specialist knowledge and
skills are understandably at a premium. However, it is worth
noting that the study boundaries and the changes in emphases were
introduced only after lengthy discussions between academics and
those actively involved in the business world. Indeed, the
redrawn parameters are to a large extent the result of pressures
on the educational system by those in business who absorb the
products of the academic mix. Concern remains - as it should.
There are those who welcome the new approach. There are those who
disapprove. Yet the case studies which follow here are related to
a development which should prove less controversial. It seems
reasonable to suggest that there should be a substantial integrative element in any course of study devised for business training.
This is the purpose of the Cross Modular Assignments in the
Business Education Council courses. Other bodies involved with
business education aim to achieve integration by alternative means,
but the need for an integrative element now seems to be widely
accepted.

One vehicle for integrating studies is the case study, which
explains what follows. A variety of inter-disciplinary problems
are posed. Like real-life business problems they are not con-
strained by study boundaries. The scenarios simulate realistic
business situations and aim both to bridge the gap between
classroom theory and real-life business problems and to integrate
the various areas of study.

The case studies are also designed to give the students an
opportunity to exercise their imaginations and this is a field of
study which could easily be overlooked in a training programme. Of
course students need to be trained in the use of appropriate techniques. One cannot go far in business without understanding
accounting conventions, the principles of demand and supply theory,
the extent of legal constraints and so on. Again, engulfed as we
are in the throes of the microprocessor revolution, anyone who
hopes to contribute to business in the future will certainly need
to be familiar with at least the functions and applications of the
computer. The greater the comprehension and facility, the greater
the chance of a successful career. However there is another side

to business. The business is an enterprise and a variety of entrepreneurial skills are called for from time to time if the organisation is to survive. In these circumstances it seems reasonable to
suggest that qualities such as vision and initiative, ingenuity
and judgement are worth cultivating. It is with these thoughts in
mind that the scenarios which follow attempt to emphasise the
entrepreneurial nature of business. The vital contribution made
by entrepreneurial skills could explain the otherwise surprising
truth that the most successful businessmen and women are not always
those with the highest academic qualifications.

A typical example of an entrepreneur in action was given by
Leslie Watkins in *The Sunday Times* of 10 January 1982 who reported:

> Orders are now pouring into one of the most unlikely factories
> in Britain - a converted cowshed in Devon. Ornate bone china
> produced in the cowshed has been bought for leading stores on
> both sides of the Atlantic, including Harrods and Neiman Marcus.
> The success vindicates the gamble taken four years ago by David
> Bowkett when he launched his business with a borrowed £10,000
> and no previous experience of making bone china. His most eye-
> catching specialities are miniature birds, retailing at between
> £60 and £220 each in limited editions which he designs and
> models. Yet the only modelling he'd done before 1978 was as a
> boy with plasticine.

In this case the entrepreneur obviously had special skills but
there is a great need for innovative thinking generally. Bear in
mind the simplest ideas often have the greatest impact on application. As a case in point consider the notion of flexible working
hours. For many years the roads into our cities were crammed with
cars and the trains and buses were over-filled with workers
striving to reach their places of work at the universally ordained
time of 9.00 a.m. A corresponding outflow was programmed to leave
for home at the magic hour of 5.30 p.m. Why not flexible working
hours whereby the employee is able to choose, within prescribed
limits, the starting and finishing times of work each day? Why not
a coretime during which workers are obliged to attend, leaving the
remaining work hours to be made up as workers feel inclined? There
is nothing complex or incomprehensible about the notion of flexible
working hours and now it is a widely accepted device for dealing
with commuting problems and domestic responsibilities. Yet a whole
generation of workers and managers suffered the stresses of un-
necessarily overcrowded roads and railways.

Another simple but effective idea propounded in recent years has
been the 'good attendance bonus'. Even in a recession many firms
face problems of absenteeism and lateness. Sociologists teach us
that people are persuaded to behave in an appropriate fashion
through the application of a system of rewards and punishments. In
Red China deviant workers are obliged to run the gauntlet of abuse
from their fellow-workers. So how do *we* reward those who do the
'right' thing and punish those who behave antisocially? What can
we expect to happen if we make no distinction? Slackers and those
who are diligent will be treated alike. To avoid this situation
some employers have introduced a bonus for those who conform. The
'good attendance bonus' is paid to those workers who attend work

regularly over a given period of time, say, a week. And such encouragement has often been found to produce the desired result. Whether or not we advocate the use of this particular remedy in a given situation it remains as one more option available to a manager seeking a suitable scourge for the tardy workers.

The worst problem facing western industrial societies at the moment is obviously unemployment. Writing in the *Observer* of 31 January 1982, Robert Taylor predicts:

> For the rest of the Eighties, Britain will have more than three million registered unemployed, if present government economic policies continue unchanged. Indeed, there seems little hope of any dramatic reduction in the numbers out of work in this country for the rest of the century, whatever any political party might like to assert.

Are there alternatives to such high levels of unemployment? If so, what are they? Earlier retirement - voluntary, or enforced? More time spent at school and college? Shorter working weeks? Work-sharing? No doubt future generations will wonder why it took us so long to surmount our difficulties when the solution was so 'obvious'.

PROBLEM-SOLVING

If what is required to deal with unemployment is innovative thinking on a grand scale, it also has an important role to play in business generally - essentially by extending the range of options available to managers dealing with the everyday problems of industry and commerce.

Peter Drucker explains why decision-making skills need to be cultivated in aspiring managers:

> Whatever a manager does he does through making decisions. Those decisions may be made as a matter of routine. Indeed, he may not even realize that he is making them. Or they may affect the future existence of the enterprise and require years of systematic analysis. But management is always a decision-making process.
> (*The Practice of Management*, Pan Books 1968)

The first stage in the decision-making process is to identify the problem. For example, a sales manager might be faced with a falling share of the market. Or a financial director might be confronted with an adverse cash flow.

Having identified the problem the next stage is to look for alternative remedies or options. In the case of a falling share of the market the sales manager's most likely options would be:

(1) increased expenditure on advertising;
(2) the introduction of an improved product (or service);
(3) an intensification of selling effort/motivation.

There may be other options. For example, it may be possible to take over the company which is encroaching or it may be possible to offer improved credit facilities. A range of options will be considered - and evaluated. What are the pros and cons of each of the options being considered? What would be the effect on costs - and on revenue - short term and long term?

Having evaluated the options a decision will have to be made as to which of the alternatives is preferred.

The final stage in the decision-making process will be to implement the decision - to put it into effect - and to monitor the results taking corrective action in the event of deviations occurring.

While the frameworks provided by the case studies can help students develop decision-making skills, training in the implementation of business decisions can only come through experience. However decision-making is a normal part of business life. Peter Fearns explains:

> Decision-making is an everyday occurrence for everyone. We decide what to eat, what to wear, when to go out, and so on. Similarly decisions are part of an organisation's everyday activities. Routine tasks, by their very nature, exclude the employee from the decision-making process, but middle and top management will be using their judgement every day. The higher one goes in the hierarchy, the more necessary is the skill of decision-making. People at the top of an organisation are employed to have initiative - to make decisions. For example, boards of directors are employed to make policy decisions in investment, manpower and marketing. The risks which all organisations face mean that organisations have to be run by people who have the ability to diagnose and assess the risk, and the capacity to decide on the correct strategy. Business is constantly changing and organisations require people with enterprise and initiative in order to survive.
> (*Business Studies: an Integrated Approach*; Hodder & Stoughton, 1980)

Students will find an ideal environment in business is one where their decision-making skills are developed by stages and the problem-solving practice obtained from the case study work herein can be seen as a means of facilitating progress at all stages of the executive's career. In the work situation, however, managers will find succour from two very different sources.

The computer
The first commercially available business computer was installed for the purpose of data processing at the US Bureau of the Census in 1951. It was retired to the Smithsonian Institution in 1964. Succeeding generations of computers have become cheaper and smaller. The effect on the role of the decision-makers can be gleaned from an article by Guy de Jonquieres in the *Financial Times* of 18 January 1982:

> The computer today can perform, in seconds, those operations which would have once required thousands of man hours to carry out, or which it would have been physically impossible to do at all. It can compress into a space, occupying only a medium-sized

room, volumes of information which would fill several libraries
if committed to paper. And it can retrieve, order, and cross
reference them at speeds which would defeat a regiment of lib-
rarians . . . The arrival of the personal computer ushers in the
same personal freedom as did the mass-produced motor car. It
offers the individual greatly-expanded choice and control,
bringing to his desktop processing power and data storage
capacity which a few years ago would have been available only
in a large computer. Moreover, it is available on demand.

It is obvious that such facilities can provide managers with an
enhanced flow of information which enables them to improve the
quality of their decisions. It is not simply the volume of data
available which allows this. It is also the ease of retrieval
and the speed and accuracy of calculations which is possible.
   One of the technological aids likely to be increasingly available to management is the computer-linked word processor by
means of which, *inter alia*, letters, reports and other documents
can be originated, edited, revised, altered in format and reproduced at speed. Any such aids facilitate the decision-making process but there are warning signs that managerial prerogatives will
be eroded increasingly.

Idea exchange
There is still another form of aid available to the manager in the
role of decision-maker. The value of high technology is indisput-
able but there are also advantages to be gained by consulting
other people in the organisation with a view to pooling and
exchanging ideas. A manager is judged on the results achieved.
Results are achieved through people. The board of directors will
need to motivate their managing director to achieve the targets
they set for that person. If the managing director reaches these
goals it will be through the efforts of the senior executives
in the management hierarchy. In turn the senior executives are
dependent upon the efforts of their work teams. In the final
analysis, sales are made over the shop counters. Motor cars are
produced on the factory floor. Dale S. Beach sums up the situation
as follows:

   Participation is the term used to designate the process by which
   people contribute ideas toward the solution of problems affecting
   the organisation and their jobs. The people exercise some degree
   of influence on the decision-making process. Participation is
   ego and task involvement of an individual or group. It includes
   not only the physical contribution of the person but also his
   intellectual and emotional involvement in the affairs of the
   organisation. When managers establish means, on either an informal or formal basis, for obtaining help from subordinates in
   the making of plans and decisions, they are tapping the knowledge and creativity of others. Because managers can't possibly
   know all the answers to all the problems and issues connected
   with the work of their departments, they can often obtain
   valuable advice and assistance from their subordinates. The
   process of participation brings into play the higher drives and

motives of man: the drives for self-expression, accomplishment,
autonomy, and self-assertion. It lets the employees know that
their contributions are sought and appreciated. Great benefits
to the company and its members can derive from such leadership;
however, participation is not a cure-all nor necessarily the
most appropriate style of management for all circumstances.
(*Personnel: the Management of People at Work,* 2nd edn, Collier-
Macmillan, 1970)

Aspiring managers could be well advised therefore to develop a
capacity for expressing points of view, contributing ideas,
querying other people's proposals in a polite and constructive
manner, so that they can prove themselves to be dynamic and
valuable members of the team. The benefits are twofold. On the
one hand they are indulging in what can be described as one of the
less painful and more effective learning experiences, while on the
other hand, they are preparing themselves for their future managerial roles.

OBJECTIVES AND PARAMETERS
Decision-making requires direction. That is to say, before an
appropriate choice can be made between options available it has to
be known what we are attempting to achieve. To what goal or goals
are our efforts to be directed - and to what extent are parameters
or boundaries prescribed for us? At one level it could be said
that the purpose of the decision-maker in business will be either
to achieve a given result with the minimum expenditure of resources,
or to achieve maximum profits from a given allocation of resources.
Profits are seen by some as antisocial, yet, given the strictures
of a mixed economy, profits become the bedrock of the affluent
society and the cornerstone on which the superstructure of the
welfare state rests. If businesses make profits, and those profits
are substantially taxed by the government, the taxes collected
can be spent on roads, hospitals, education, old-age pensions and
welfare generally. Conversely, a contraction of profits reduces
the flow of taxes and, inevitably, the flow of benefits.
However, in a pluralist industrial society a business executive
may be faced with a quite complex battery of objectives and constraints. The complexities are admirably defined in the philosophy
of Trusthouse Forte Plc as published in their *Reports and Accounts*:

The company philosophy
To increase profitability and earnings per share each year in
order to encourage investment and to improve and expand the
business.

To give complete customer satisfaction by efficient and courteous
service with value for money.

To support managers and their staff in using personal initiative
to improve the profit and quality of their operations whilst
observing the company's policies.

To provide good working conditions and to maintain effective
communications at all levels to develop better understanding
and assist decision-making.

To ensure no discrimination against sex, race, colour or creed and to train, develop and encourage promotion within the company based on merit and ability.

To act with integrity at all times and to maintain a proper sense of responsibility towards the public.

To recognise the importance of each and every employee who contributes towards these aims.

Some might be critical of such a statement of intent on the grounds that they are vague or ambiguous. Others, with experience of the ruggedness and competitiveness of business life, might dismiss such ideals as spurious. And yet there is historical evidence that scrupulously fair dealing might be the most logical approach - in the long run. Some of the early Quakers became very successful traders. Why? It seems they dressed distinctively and were easily identified. And they did not attempt to take advantage of those with whom they traded. So those travellers who wanted to trade sought out the Quakers and confidently traded with them. The Quakers' businesses flourished. On this evidence business integrity might still provide us with the best available yardstick for long-term profitability.

THE PURPOSE OF WHAT FOLLOWS

In the light of what has been suggested so far, the material which follows is intended to furnish a series of simulated business scenarios incorporating a selection of typical problems such as might confront managers in a variety of companies, in a variety of industries, at various stages of development. The specific aims are:

(1) to bridge the gap between classroom theory and real-life business situations;
(2) to interrelate the various discipline or subject areas in a typical business studies course;
(3) to provide vehicles for discussion where students are able to function in groups; and
(4) to give the students an opportunity to develop analytic and decision-making skills.

From the tutors' point of view, by using the *addendum technique* referred to in *Introducing Business Studies: a Case Study and Assignment Approach* (Macmillan, 1979) it would be possible to add further material to any of the scenarios so as to augment or adapt the learning package as required. Conversely, it should prove simple enough to omit those aspects of a case deemed less critical with regard to a particular course of study.

1.   Talisman Technics

Stefan Schornberg spent three years with an electronics firm after
graduating. His elder brother Gregor had meanwhile spent his time
and energy researching in laser technology at one of the major
universities in the United States. When they met up again in
London last year they had a lot of ideas to exchange and before
long they were working out a scheme to market their brainchild -
an ingenious and comparatively cheap security device. The principle is simple enough. A set of specially devised sensors are
placed in the four corners of the room to be secured. It was
Stefan's artistic talents which were unleashed when he produced
designs for a series of porcelain ornaments ranging from tradition-
al flower vases and cupid figures to decidedly futuristic space-
ships. The sensory devices are embedded in these figures which
are then fixed into the walls. The power required is minimal and
is provided by miniature batteries which are also slotted into the
ornaments. If there is any movement in the room once the sensors
have been switched on an alarm is activated.

Though not yet ready for production on a large scale, an
industrial model has also been developed - without the ornaments -
and in this case the sensors are actually embedded in the wall
plaster. A stronger 'ray' is emitted and this is linked to the
telephone switchboard. If the ray is broken at any time a signal
will be received at the local police station.

It is not only the police who are showing interest in the idea.
The army have also asked to see the device demonstrated. But the
problem at this stage for the Schornberg brothers is to market the
domestic model as effectively as possible. Stefan has undertaken
some basic market research in South Yorkshire where they intend
to concentrate their marketing effort (they are natives of
Barnsley) and has provided the following statistics shown in
Table 1.1.

All prices and costs quoted are for complete security systems
comprising four sensory units with batteries and wall plaques, and
quotations include installation costs. All estimates are on a
twelve-monthly basis. Stefan feels that longer-term forecasts will
need to be adjusted in the light of experience.

Draw a graph to record the level of output and sales at which
the Schornbergs would break even, on this evidence.

The sales force
As you may appreciate by now Stefan tends to be the businessman in
this outfit while Gregor is more interested in the technical

TABLE 1.1

Sales forecast							
Domestic model	Price	£200	£300	£400	£500	£600	£700
	Estimated Sales	7000	4000	2500	1500	1000	500

Estimated production costs (in £000s): levels of output (in units/systems)

Level of output	1000	2000	3000	4000	5000	6000	7000
Fixed costs	500	500	500	500	500	500	500
Variable costs	50	100	150	200	250	300	350
Semi-variable costs	100	175	200	250	255	240	500
Total costs	650	775	850	950	1005	1040	1350

problems. But both brothers realise that a great deal of skill and effort is going to be required to market their security systems at the prices they are hoping for. Stefan has estimated from his brief experience to date that an enthusiastic salesman could be expected to sell twelve domestic or five industrial systems a week. But as Gregor reminded his brother when they got round to this subject recently, any salesman in this operation would need to inspire the customer with confidence. In Stefan's own words, 'If I had anything worth safeguarding I wouldn't want to talk about it to some shifty character who looks as if he's just come out of prison.'

Stefan took the point and had another look at the advertisement he had prepared for insertion in the local newspaper.

High Bonuses for Ambitious Salesmen

A fantastic opportunity to join a small but dynamic concern selling a revolutionary type of security equipment (patents applied for). The market is local initially but will become nationwide within months.

High rates of commission will give keen sales representatives the chance to earn in excess of £20,000 a year.

For an early interview telephone Stefan Schornberg at 337265. Interviews will take place at the Crown Hotel, Cranbourne, on Thursday and Friday next week.

Stefan does not underrate the importance of selecting his salesmen with care. He has sketched out a profile of the ideal salesman he would like to employ. He has drawn a job specification chart relating to five aspects of the individuals he expects to be interviewing (see Figure 1.1).

You will see from this chart that Stefan feels that the most important quality he is looking for is a high level of motivation. There are ten points on each of the extending bars and Stefan has assessed the need for motivation well above average - at point eight in fact. The other aspects are regarded as much less important. Indeed he feels the sales representatives require less than average frustration tolerance as registered under the heading of Adjustment. In his view, the salesmen will move on to the next customer whenever they find themselves meeting sales resistance. Gregor suggested that the salesman would need to be endowed with a considerable amount of patience, but Stefan does not agree. You will see that he has given Adjustment only a four-point rating - below average. What are your views?

Write a brief profile of your own under the headings shown in

the job specification indicating the sort of person the Schorn-
berg brothers should be looking for as sales representatives.

FIGURE 1.1

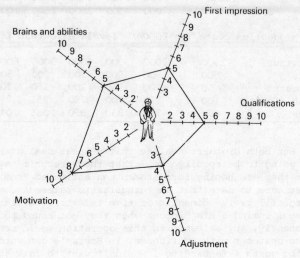

The finance and control of the project
The brothers have decided to form a limited company, Talisman
Technics Ltd, each taking 50% of the ordinary shares which will
carry one vote each. They subscribed £1 for each of the shares
allocated. Gregor has provided an additional £15,000 and has been
allocated unsecured debenture stock redeemable ten years after the
date of issue. The company's opening balance sheet will take on
the following shape shown in Table 1.2.

TABLE 1.2

Capital and liabilities		Assets		
	(£)			(£)
Authorised and issued capital		Freehold workshop		117,000.00
Ordinary shares of £1 each	125,000.00	Equipment		68,200.00
12% redeemable debentures	15,000.00	Fixed Assets		185,200.00
Creditors	10,757.75	Stock	1,257.75	
Bank loan	40,000.00	Bank balance	4,200.00	
		Current assets		5,457.75
		Patents		100.00
	£190,757.75			£190,757.75

Notes:
1 The bank have also agreed to give the company overdraft facilities up to a limit of £75,000 over the next six months. They

10

have taken as security a deposit of the property deeds on equitable mortgage.

2 The bank have also taken as security the personal guarantee of Paul Schornberg, the father of Gregor and Stefan, against any debts incurred by the company. The father is a wealthy indust-rialist, being a principal shareholder in a West Midlands company which manufactures a wide range of the more expensive chinaware.

Differences of opinion are bound to arise between the members of the family from time to time. What problems would you envisage developing in the long run in this set-up?

Advertising the new security system
Stefan plans to advertise the Talisman System through the medium of local newspapers. He plans to advertise in six or seven succes-sive editions in one locality before moving on to the next. He has drafted the sort of advertisement he is thinking of using - within a 15 x 10 cm block (see Figure 1.2). He accepts that this could be greatly improved and is toying with a variety of presentations.

FIGURE 1.2

PROTECTION
with style

SWAG

Easily Fitted

ELECTRONIC DETECTIVE

DID YOU KNOW that 60,000 people were convicted of BURGLARY last year? And over 50% of those convicted were under 17?

Does it make you feel uncomfortable?

Why not use modern technology to solve your security problems. At Talisman Technics we have invented an electronic miracle — a magic eye which will give you warning whenever an intruder appears.

If you have valuables you want to protect at home or in the office or factory why not contact us and let us set up for you an infallible high-technology security system?

If you want to relax in your own home — if you want to sleep in peace — knowing that your property is adequately protected, complete the coupon below and send it to:

Talisman Technics Ltd, P.O. Box 35, Barnsley.

Name ....
Address ....
....
....

What changes would you suggest? Design an advertisement which you feel would be more appropriate and effective.

11

YOUR FINAL ASSIGNMENT
Play the role of the newly appointed personal assistant to Stefan
Schornberg. He has asked you to consider the various aspects of
the new project as outlined here and report to him the major
problems you see confronting the company in the short and medium
terms. A report of 600-800 words is called for.

2. The Downhill Run

Charlton-Chester Plc is a public company sited on the outskirts of
Downhill. It has enjoyed a long history of manufacturing and selling high-quality bicycles with a reputation for easy riding and
durability. They have been particularly successful in overseas
markets, notably in South East Asia. Unfortunately for the company there has been increasing competition in this market in recent
years and their share of the market has fallen dramatically. There
has been a compensatory boom in the domestic market but the annual
accounts have shown losses for the past two years and no ordinary
dividend has been paid for the past three years.

In an effort to stimulate sales a new bicycle has been developed.
It is called the *Challenger* and has the following special features:

(1)   an extra light and low-slung alloy frame;
(2)   twin fork legs to which is attached a weatherproof plastic-
      coated metal pannier;
(3)   smaller wheels - front and rear - fitted with wide-tread
      tyres and a new suspension system which is reckoned to make
      it easier to ride under all conditions.

Both the sales manager and the production manager have confidence
in the new machine. But it has been necessary to cut back overall
production at Downhill and two of the existing models will have to
be phased out so that the *Challenger* production line can be set up.
The following models are included in their existing range of
bicycles:

Cheetah   a lightweight sports model with many of the features of
the more expensive racing cycles. 80% of the sales have been
recorded in the domestic market.
Chickadee   a folding bike with a special foam saddle designed to
optimise comfort. 65% of the sales have been in the home market.
Chesapeake   a heavy service machine but with five speed gears,
metal mudguards and chainguards. Sells particularly well in East
Africa and India. 40% of sales are to these areas.
Chieftain   has a low-slung frame and high-rise handlebars, a rear
saddle bag and front-wheel shock absorbers. This has tended to be
the most popular model for overseas purchasers. Since it was first
introduced 90% of all sales have been to the Far East.

To help management to decide which of the existing models to
drop, the sales department has produced details of sales of each
up to the end of September last (see Table 2.1).
*You are asked to work out appropriate moving averages with a
view to determining trends. On this evidence you are called to*

make a decision as to which of the two existing models should be abandoned in favour of the new Challenger.

TABLE 2.1 Sales in sterling over past 21 months (in £s million)

	Cheetah		Chickadee		Chesapeake		Chieftain	
	Yr 1	Yr 2	Yr 1	Yr 2	Yr 1	Yr 2	Yr 1	Yr 2
Jan	2.27	2.09	2.16	2.32	2.86	2.59	3.21	2.46
Feb	2.56	1.97	2.08	2.01	2.34	2.56	3.08	2.35
Mar	2.51	2.29	2.18	1.96	2.42	2.32	3.00	2.29
Apr	2.82	2.48	2.09	2.01	2.60	2.34	2.96	2.40
May	2.67	2.25	2.31	2.00	2.57	2.19	2.94	2.26
Jun	2.58	2.17	2.45	1.96	2.43	2.24	2.86	2.19
Jul	2.67	2.32	2.95	2.34	2.27	1.96	2.79	2.10
Aug	2.12	2.04	2.07	1.65	2.19	1.87	2.82	1.95
Sep	2.68	2.39	2.16	2.00	2.24	2.03	2.75	1.86
Oct	2.09		2.08		2.37		2.63	
Nov	1.95		2.12		2.47		2.54	
Dec	2.49		2.42		2.58		2.47	

Market research
The sales manager is aware that new designs will need to be forth-coming to meet the changing requirements of the market and is developing a questionnaire which he is hoping to submit to dealers in Hong Kong and Malaysia. He has given an indication of the sort of question he wants the dealers to answer in the survey.

To. (Name of dealer)

. . . . (Address)

It is our aim to make selling our bicycles as pleasant and profitable as possible. We are most anxious to find out your views on a number of important issues and wonder whether you would be so kind as to answer the questions below. If you will return the completed questionnaire to us with your next communication we shall be able to consider your replies and gear our operations accordingly.

Charlton-Chester Plc
J. Corrigan
Sales Manager

Please place ticks in the appropriate boxes.

1. Which of the frame colours in the present range is most popular? Lime Green ☐ Emerald Green ☐ Cambridge ☐ Blue ☐ Oxford Blue ☐ Canary Yellow ☐ Scarlet ☐ Royal Purple ☐ Bright Orange ☐
2. Would a dynamo lighting set as an optional extra be attractive at a price between £7 and £8.50?
    Very attractive ☐ Fairly attractive ☐ Not attractive ☐
3. How much extra would your customers be prepared to pay for a foam saddle as offered on the Chickadee?
    £5-£6 ☐ £6-£7 ☐ £7-£8 ☐ £8-£9 ☐ £9-£10 ☐

You are invited to improve the questionnaire and add a selection of further questions with appropriate responses bearing in mind that the dealers will not want to be unduly burdened with an over-long questionnaire. (Use your imagination but aim to make your questions as useful as possible to find out as much as possible about the prospective market.)

The problem of redundancies
Management have notified the unions involved at Downhill that 15% of the workforce will be made redundant in three months while a further 10% of the remaining workers will lose their jobs six months later. It has been agreed that the unions will draw up formal recommendations for a policy for redundancy which will be acceptable to their side. To aid them in their deliberations they have been provided with the statistics shown in Tables 2.2 and 2.3.

TABLE 2.2 Present downhill workforce analysed by age/sex and length of service

		Under 2 years	2-5 years	6-10 years	Over 10 years
Under 21	M	552	80	–	–
	F	201	32	–	–
21-30 years	M	123	127	477	
	F	124	13	3	–
31-40 years	M	68	115	406	502
	F	29	35	17	12
41-50 years	M	68	125	229	396
	F	5	8	3	–
Over 50	M	–	7	74	299
	F	–	–	14	42

TABLE 2.3 Present downhill workforce analysed by department and age/sex (with supervisors in brackets)

		Assembly	Pressing	Spraying	Stores	Inspection and testing
Under 21	M	494	119	19	–	–
	F	199	–	–	34	–
21-30	M	593 (29)	59 (2)	43	23	9
	F	137 (2)	–	–	3	–
31-40	M	624 (83)	385 (20)	43 (8)	15 (7)	24
	F	76 (5)	–	–	6 (1)	11
41-50	M	172 (21)	398 (64)	197 (15)	11 (4)	40 (7)
	F	7 (3)	–	–	8 (3)	1 (1)
Over 50	M	121 (47)	161 (24)	11 (8)	39 (9)	48 (15)
	F	13 (5)	2	–	39	2 (1)

Management have pointed out to the trade unions that 90% of all job losses will take place in the assembly department. It is in this section of the works that the production lines for the four existing models are set up. The new production line for the *Challenger* will be fully automated (or computerised). The shop steward's committee refer to the company 'bringing in the robots'.

You are asked to play the role of the trade union representatives and working together your task is to draw up a plan sketching out your proposals for the proposed redundancies. Attempt to reach a consensus.

The personnel department has produced charts covering the last three calendar years in the hope that they will help you in your deliberations (see Figures 2.1 and 2.2).

FIGURE 2.1   Employees leaving the company other than through retirement

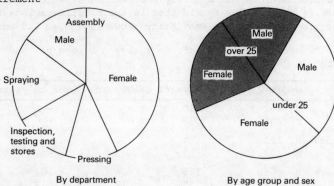

By department   By age group and sex

FIGURE 2.2   Total number of employees leaving the company other than through retirement

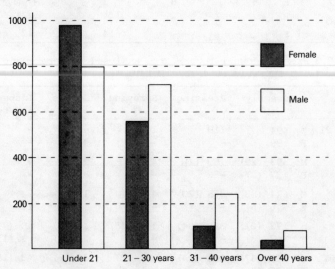

Your final assignment is to reproduce the charts in alternative forms.

16

3.   A Tiger in your Tank

Some years ago a major international oil company conducted an
advertising campaign which suggested that when you bought their
petrol it was equivalent to putting a tiger in the tank of your
car. T. Eiger (Fruit Drinks) Ltd is now using the same slogan but
this time it is their fruit drinks which young people are being
encouraged to buy. The drinks are made up of various fruit juices
but they are vitamin enriched and so - according to the accom-
panying advertising material - a drink of Teiger (pronounced
tiger) will help them to break world records in every sport from
mountaineering to long-distance running.

The Eiger company is a subsidiary of one of Britain's largest
breweries. It was incorporated two years ago as part of a larger
programme of decentralisation aimed at giving various divisions in
the group a greater degree of autonomy. The brewery had been
achieving numerous economies as a result of their increasingly
large scale of operations but they had been running up against all
sorts of managerial difficulties - including an inexplicably
militant workforce. Jonathan Cutforth had been appointed the first
Managing Director of the company and had been given four specific
targets:

(1)   To achieve an annual level of profit as determined by the
      Chairman who is also a member of the board of directors for
      the holding company.
(2)   To limit capital expenditure in accordance with the annual
      budget as approved by the Chairman.
(3)   To achieve a significant level of sales in overseas territor-
      ies during a five-year period.
(4)   To improve the morale of the workforce and persuade them to
      attain significantly higher levels of performance during a
      five-year period.

During Jonathan Cutforth's first two years in office he has
been concentrating his efforts on the physical and financial
targets, but he is now giving attention to the problems of the
workforce in his organisation. He has been provided with certain
figures by his personnel manager (see Tables 3.1, 3.2 and 3.3)
and has asked for a special meeting with the board of directors
at which he intends to present a paper on how industrial relations
might be improved.

He has five specific schemes in mind as outlined below:

TABLE 3.1   Absenteeism/lateness/turnover on bottling and labelling lines

---

Processes involved (fully automated, large batch production)
Line 1:   plastic bottle manufacture.
Line 2:   cardboard carton manufacture, plastic lined.
Line 3:   filling and labelling machines.

Workers analysed by age

		under 21	21-30	31-40	41-50	51-60	over 60
Numbers employed (average)							
first year	M	24	19	16	13	9	7
	F	27	22	18	11	7	0
last year	M	21	23	25	8	5	0
	F	30	30	19	3	0	0
Days lost through absenteeism							
first year	M	296	181	111	83	66	59
	F	601	312	132	84	34	-
last year	M	334	259	236	81	30	-
	F	789	428	129	13	-	-
Times late							
first year	M	387	101	76	87	59	31
	F	657	214	74	61	36	-
last year	M	437	225	89	90	52	-
	F	838	390	49	11	-	-
Workers leaving company							
first year	M	15	5	6	7	2	2
	F	35	11	3	2	4	0
last year	M	27	9	8	3	2	0
		59	23	2	2	3	0

TABLE 3.2   Absenteeism/lateness/turnover on mixing bays

Process involved: fruit juices and additives mixed in 2000 litre vats which are then fed into the production lines. The workforce is all male. There are two shifts a day - the 6 a.m. shift is double-manned.

	first year	last year
Average number employed	43	45
Days lost through absenteeism	936	984
Times late	101	123
Workers leaving company	7	8

TABLE 3.3   Absenteeism/lateness/turnover of office and sales staff

Work done: accounts, wages, secretarial, selling, marketing, etc.

		first year	last year
Average number employed	M	28	29
	F	24	24
Days absent	M	402	431
	F	469	488
Staff leaving	M	4	6
	F	11	14

A. Workers' shares
All workers who have been with the company for more than two years
will be given an option to purchase a certain number of shares
(related to their length of service) at a future date and at a pre-
determined price. Thus if the value of the shares rises in the
meantime they will exercise their option to buy the shares but
will only be required to pay the price for the shares as it stands
now. To pay for the shares employees will save an agreed amount
from their pay packet every month for a period of five years. One
of the problems with this scheme is that T. Eiger (Fruit Drinks)
Ltd shares are not quoted on a stock exchange, but the holding
company does have a stock exchange quotation for its shares.
   However the scheme should be popular with the workers because
(a) they only need to exercise their option to buy shares if the
price goes up in the meantime, (b) a 10% discount is offered on
the price regardless of where it stands at the option date and
(c) interest will be earned on the savings as they build up -
they will be invested in the government's Save As You Earn scheme.

B. Works council
A works council will be formed to consider matters of importance
affecting the workforce - wage negotiations being specifically
excluded. The council will consist of three members of management
and twelve members of the workforce elected by their workmates in
each department. The first task to be undertaken by the council
will be to work out a Constitution for the company setting out
the rights and obligations of all employees. Grievance and dispute
procedures will also be set up as soon as possible. Other matters
which are envisaged as falling within the purview of the council
are:

(a) canteen management,
(b) social functions,
(c) organisation of staff magazine, and
(d) safety publicity.

It is not intended that the works council will supersede the shop
stewards' committee. Rather it will deal with the many topics
which are not of particular interest to the committee. The works
manager meets regularly with the shop stewards and will continue
to do so. Being involved with both groups of representatives he

will be able to ensure there is minimal overlapping.

The works council will meet once a month. The Chairman will be the works manager (or his deputy). Normal committee routines will be followed, but the resolutions passed will be deemed as advisory to management or unions. 82% of the workforce are members of one or other of the five unions represented in the Eiger factories.

C. A good-timekeeping bonus

When the next round of pay increases is negotiated an attempt will be made to make a substantial portion of the increase as dependent upon satisfactory attendance and punctuality. It is envisaged that a sum of, say, £5 per week will be paid to the employee only when during a given week he has not been absent or late for either a morning or an afternoon period.

The present arrangements are that any employee who is late loses a minimum of half an hour's pay and any member of staff with more than two years' service is given full pay for the first month of absence. Those with less than two years' service are not compensated for absence.

An additional feature of the scheme proposed is that all employees who are not absent or late for a period of three months are included in a list from which three prize-winners are selected by lot. Each will receive a prize of £75 in Premium Savings Bonds. Photos of prize-winners will be displayed in magazines.

D. Removal of management-worker barriers

Note has been taken of some of the practices of Japanese managements operating in the United Kingdom and as a result certain changes will be implemented as and when possible, in particular:

(1) a uniform overall in dark blue with the Eiger crest emblazoned on the breast pocket will be worn by *all* employees while on normal duties within the plant. Underneath the crest a small oblong patch will give the name of the employee and an appropriate job title, e,g, Plant Manager or Storekeeper, The name will include a first name.
(2) The existing partition which separates the workers' canteen from the executive and office staff canteen will be removed. Managers and machine operators, secretaries and cleaners will in future share the same canteen and enjoy the same menus and facilities.
(3) Only plant workers are required to clock on and off at present but in future all employees, including managers and office staff, will be required to clock on and off.

E. Job enrichment

The personnel department will look at the design of all existing jobs on the factory floor with a view to making jobs more interesting/less boring wherever possible. Where job designs cannot be improved to alleviate the effects of boredom efforts will be made to redesign work-flows with a view to clustering workers on production lines so that they can work together in small cohesive teams. Wherever possible meaningful targets will be set for individuals/groups with the purpose of stimulating enthusiasm. Competition will be encouraged between the various groups.

YOUR ASSIGNMENT
The board of directors of T. Eiger (Soft Drinks) Ltd are meeting to consider these proposals and the Managing Director has asked you to evaluate them. To do this draw up a list of merits and demerits for eacn of the proposals. You are also invited to suggest a rank order for the five different schemes, indicating which are likely to be most and least effective in your view and on the evidence available.

OTHER QUESTIONS TO CONSIDER
1. If the board of directors generally disapprove of one or other of the schemes proposed by the managing director, what action do you think they should take? If constraints are to be placed on the chief executive in a situation like this, how do you think they should be applied?
2. Subsidiaries of T. Eiger (Fruit Drinks) Ltd are to be set up in Nigeria and Malaysia within the next six months. To what extent do you think personnel policies such as those discussed here should be imposed on the new organisations? How do you think control might be exercised by the holding company over its subsidiaries?

AN ADDITIONAL ASSIGNMENT
Interpret the statistics shown in Tables 3.1 to 3.3 diagramatically in a form which would be helpful to the board of directors in their deliberations.

4.   M. S. Mardi Gras

The Mardi Gras is one of the smaller luxury passenger liners in
one of the world's major shipping fleets. It has carried a total
of a hundred thousand passengers on a variety of cruises since
it was launched fifteen years ago but it is now in dry dock being
generally overhauled and modernised. This operation is planned
to last six months and when it resumes service it will have three
spacious sun-decks, a swimming pool, two games areas and a ship's
video library. There will be facilities for shuffle-board, quoits,
deck tennis, table tennis and clay pigeon shooting. Meanwhile 80%
of the crew and staff have been dispersed to other ships in the
fleet and approximately 20% have been paid off while the owners
are considering the future role of the Mardi Gras. Being smaller
than some of the other vessels in the fleet it has proved to be
slightly less profitable, though the cabin occupancy has averaged
76% on voyages during the past two years which is above average
for the fleet.

Until now the Mardi Gras has been used principally on the London-
Madeira-Canary Islands run with an annual tour of the Mediterranean.
It has proved a very popular craft with both crew and passengers,
most of whom comment that being a smaller ship than many others
performing the same sort of task, there is a friendlier atmosphere on board. Passengers in the past have complained about
excessive roll in heavy seas but anti-roll mechanisms are being
introduced during the refitting programme. However the owners are
looking at the widest possible range of options. A number of ideas
are already under consideration: one proposal is that the Mardi
Gras should operate exclusively on world cruises catering for the
elderly - on the basis of 'See the world before I die'. A variation would be world education cruises in which case the Mardi
Gras would be fitted out as a floating university. In either of
these cases the refitting programme would need to be modified but
this would not present difficulties at this stage.

Another idea put forward by the Chairman of the company which
owns the Mardi Gras is that voyage time shares might be offered
for sale to the public. This would require purchasers to pay a
capital sum now which would give them the right to utilise a
particular cabin for a set period in the year. Voyages would be
arranged to cover four weeks (less time for changeovers). Insurance cover would be taken out so that the purchaser of a time
share would be compensated if a voyage was unable to take place
as a result of damage sustained by the ship. The purchasers of
voyage time shares would have purchased a proportionate share of
a fully furnished cabin which they would be able to use personally,

rent, exchange, sell at a later stage or even pass on to their
heirs. Of course there are special problems with a voyage time
share. First, there is a need to pay the crew's wages: this
amounts to about £1.5 million annually in the case of the Mardi
Gras. Then there is the problem of food and entertainment. Finally,
and by no means least, is the cost of repairs to the ship and its
furnishings. The Chairman has mentioned thirty years as an
appropriate term before the rights revert fully to the shipowners and
substantial repairs are likely to prove necessary before then.

However, as the Chairman has explained to his directors: 'There's
a lot of money being made by property owners with the time-
sharing idea and I don't see why we shouldn't get in on the act.
Anyway, I'd like you to think over the possibilities of extending
time-sharing to the cruise business. The refit of the Mardi Gras
gives us the time and the opportunity to work something out.'

He has given some indications of how the problems might be
sorted out. He envisages the formation of a management company
to cope with the supply of a crew, the provision of food and
entertainments and the organisation of voyages generally. The
owners of the time shares would also be given shares in the
management company to give them a say in the conduct of its affairs.

Other information relating to the voyage time-share proposals as
given by the Chairman:

Time-share exchange
The management company would become a member of an international
time-share network so that on purchasing a voyage time share on
the Mardi Gras the owner would join a reciprocal exchange programme entitling him to buy, sell or exchange time-share holidays
all over the world. Premiums would be payable to equalise values.
Voyage time (in four-week blocks) might be sold by the owner
personally or with the aid of the management company.

Victualling
The management company would not be expected to make a profit. The
company would be responsible for providing meals - breakfast,
lunch and dinner. Prices would be set to cover costs only. The
costs would also be partially defrayed by bar profits and the
rents (concessions) received from the leasing of the five shop
units situated on the boat deck. It has yet to be decided what
constraints to place on the leasings. It is assumed that none of
the services provided would need to be duplicated. But what
services would be particularly welcome?

Entertainments
All entertainments would be free. They would be organised by the
management company and apart from those previously mentioned
would include:

(a) resident disc jockeys - for nightly discos and ship's radio
    (morning and afternoon sessions);
(b) guided tours at each major port of call;

(c) talent contests (once a voyage);
(d) fancy dress ball (once a voyage);
(e) a gambling casino (games vary nightly) - non-profit making.

TABLE 4.1   Proposed cruises rotating over 13-year period

Weeks	Description of cruise	Main ports of call
1-4	Caribbean	Hamilton (Bermuda)-Kingston (Jamaica)-San Juan (Puerto Rico)-Port of Spain (Trinidad)
5-8	Scandinavia	Bergen-Oslo-Copenhagen-Stockholm-Helsinki-Malmo
9-12	East Africa	Lisbon-Palermo-Alexandria-Aden-Seychelles-Mombasa-Zanzibar
13-16	North America	Corner Brook (Newfoundland)-Quebec-New York-Charleston-Jacksonville
17-20	North Africa	Tangier-Algiers-Valetta (Malta)-Tunis-Oran-Casablanca
21-24	South America	Las Palmas-Cape Verde-Georgetown-Cayenne-Recife-Rio de Janeiro
25-28	West Africa	Dakar-Freetown-Monrovia-Accra-Port Harcourt (Nigeria)-Banjul (Gambia)
29-32	Eastern Mediterranean	Limassol (Cyprus)-Canea (Crete)
33-36	Pacific	Freeport (Bahamas)- Panama-Acapulco (Mexico)-Los Angeles
37-40	Italy	Genoa-Elba-Naples-Reggio-Bari-Ancona-Venice-Ravenna-Taranto-Messina
41-44	Southern States	Hamilton (Bermuda)-Savannah-Miami-Cape Canaveral (Florida)-New Orleans
45-48	Western Mediterranean	Ajaccio-Cagliari-Palma (Balearic Islands)
49-52	Rest/no cruise	

Note: The rotation of voyages means that the purchaser of weeks 1-4, say cabin 3 (upper deck see Figure 4.1), will go to the Caribbean in the first year, Scandinavia in the second year, East Africa in the third year and so on. In the thirteenth year, on this basis, there will be no cruise available for this particular time-share owner. This will be the time when repairs to the vessel take place.

FIGURE 4.1 M. S. Mardi Gras

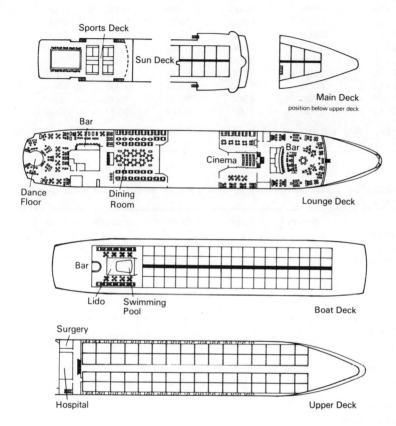

Main Deck: 14 larger cabins (with portholes).
Boat Deck: 34 smaller outer cabins (with portholes); 34 smaller
  inner cabins.
Upper Deck: 32 standard outer cabins (with portholes); 32 standard
  inner cabins.

TABLE 4.2   Costs (£s) per cabin for voyage time shares (30-year term)

Weeks	Main deck	Upper deck Inner	Outer	Boat deck Inner	Outer
1-4	7500	5000	6000	4000	5000
5-8	7500	5000	6000	4000	5000
9-12	8000	5500	6500	4500	5500
13-16	8000	5500	6500	4500	5500
17-20	8500	6000	7000	5000	6000
21-24	8500	6000	7000	5000	6000
25-28	10500	7500	8500	6500	7500
29-32	10500	7500	8500	6500	7500
33-36	10500	7500	8500	6500	7500
37-40	8000	5500	6500	4500	5500
41-44	8000	5500	6500	4500	5500
45-48	7000	4500	5500	3500	4500
49-52	7500	5000	6000	4000	5000

Note: All cabins are 2 berth and these prices pertain to occupancy by either one or two people.

TABLE 4.3   Costs/revenue attributed to Mardi Gras over past 5 years (£000s)

	Year 1	Year 2	Year 3	Year 4	Year 5 (last year)
Revenue					
Cruise bookings	2127	2247	1638	2197	2036
Bar profits/ concessions	98	77	81	72	70
Costs					
Crew's pay	1019	1186	1301	1355	1486
Fuel/ harbour dues	179	181	182	185	188
Victuals	189	209	158	212	214
Overheads incl. depreciation	255	260	268	280	302
Repairs	48	51	254	44	49
Surplus/deficit	+535	+437	-444	+193	-133

YOUR ASSIGNMENT

George Harris is one of the senior executives working for the shipping line and has been asked to produce a report for the Chairman on the future of the Mardi Gras. You are his recently recruited personal assistant and he has asked you to draft a preliminary report indicating your views on the situation generally. He has already intimated that in his view the company would be well advised to sell the ship taking advantage of an offer of

$9.5 million recently made by a rival American shipping line.
Specifically you are asked to consider:
1. the range of options available;
2. the merits and pitfalls of the voyage time-share proposals;
3. an appropriate organisation chart for a ship like the Mardi
    Gras - assuming the voyage time-share scheme proceeds (in the
    words of your boss your ideas will be particularly valuable
    because they are 'uncluttered by precedents');
4. some of the legal problems which might be generated by a pur-
    suance of the voyage time-share scheme;
5. how the voyage time-shares might be marketed.

5. Ava Advertising Agency — In Tray

Tim Cheung is the proprietor and General Manager of the AVA Advertising Agency. His family live in Hong Kong but he went to college in England and stayed to gain experience in a large London advertising agency. That was about ten years ago but having had experience in the business he decided to set up his own agency, following the death of his father who left him a substantial inheritance. The AVA Advertising Agency is quite small and the total staff involved number 25, over half of whom are in their early twenties and comparatively inexperienced. At the present time the executive staff are all working in a rather overcrowded office over shops, in the centre of a town in the West London suburbs. The production staff are five miles out of town and operate from a small workshop. However within the next three months both the executive staff and the production staff will join forces in new premises on the site of a new industrial estate.

You are asked to play the role of a recently appointed personal assistant to the general manager. You are his third PA since the business was set up fifteen months ago.

The organisation chart on the wall behind the general manager's desk is shown in Figure 5.1.

FIGURE 5.1

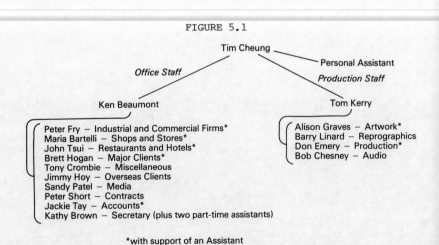

Tim Cheung

Office Staff

Personal Assistant

Production Staff

Ken Beaumont

Tom Kerry

Peter Fry — Industrial and Commercial Firms*
Maria Bartelli — Shops and Stores*
John Tsui — Restaurants and Hotels*
Brett Hogan — Major Clients*
Tony Crombie — Miscellaneous
Jimmy Hoy — Overseas Clients
Sandy Patel — Media
Peter Short — Contracts
Jackie Tay — Accounts*
Kathy Brown — Secretary (plus two part-time assistants)

Alison Graves — Artwork*
Barry Linard — Reprographics
Don Emery — Production*
Bob Chesney — Audio

*with support of an Assistant

It is a typical working day except that Mr Cheung is out of the office until next Monday. You arrive at the office and find the following items in your in-tray. You are invited to deal with them in an appropriate fashion.

Kenneth Holmes-Gardner
Certified Accountant

Tressington Chambers
Knightsbridge
London SW1X 7LB

5 January 198–

Dear Mr Cheung,

Following your recent visit I have made a first draft of your Agency's Accounts for the first year of Trading on the basis of the material you supplied. As promised I am sending you a copy forthwith.

A number of problems have emerged and I think it will be necessary to have another meeting. Would it be possible for you to visit me in the early part of next week?

Yours sincerely,

K Holmes-Gardner

ACCA

Accounts enclosed: 1 folio

Mr T Cheung
AVA Advertising Agency
Wellesley Court
London NW3 5QA

To P/A
Problems? Can you see any?
Tim Cheung

TABLE 5.1   Profit and loss account for year ending 31 March 198-.
AVA Advertising Agency

	(£)		(£)
Rent and rates	5,217	Commissions and other	
Advertising	162,372	revenue	333,560
Materials	18,665		
Salaries, etc.	93,069		
Lighting and heating	1,124		
Telephones	1,244		
Patents	300		
Travelling expenses	1,012		
Other expenses	991		
Entertaining	1,469		
Gross profit c/d	48,097		
	333,560		333,560

Balance sheet as at 31 March 198-

	(£)		(£)
Capital	80,000	Machinery at cost	48,600
add gross profit	48,097	Office equipment at cost	9,950
		Materials in stock	3,800
	128,097	Sundry debtors	137,652
less drawings	29,400	Cash at bank and in hand	651
	98,697		
Bank loan	53,333		
Creditors	48,623		
	200,653		200,653

AVA Advertising Agency

INTERNAL MEMORANDUM

To Personal Assistant

From Tim Cheung

15 January 198-

Rotary Club Lunch

On Wednesday of next week I have been invited to speak at
the Rotary Club on the subject of <u>Advertising.</u> I want to
point out that advertising plays a useful role in business
emphasising the way in which it helps to stabilise sales,
stocks, employment and prices. I have made a sketch of a
graph which indicates the sort of effect I've got in mind.
Can you check the graph for me. It would be helpful if you
could put the graph on an acetate for me because I think
an overhead projector will be available.

Also I would like you to draft a speech for me. You can
be critical of advertising too, if you wish, but I don't
want to let them think that advertising is all bad.

Tim Cheung

Graph attached [see Figure 5.2]

FIGURE 5.2

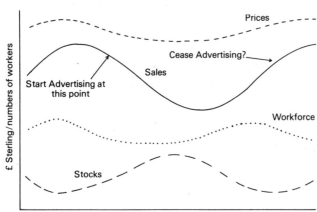

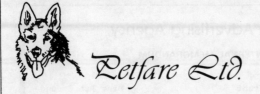

Petfare Ltd.

Toynbee Industrial Estate
Brentford

Tel 01-096-006

Ref KdC/JP   date as postmark

Dear Mr Cheung,

I was disappointed that you did not turn up to the meeting
you arranged with me for Wednesday last. My diary note
clearly shows you were to join me for lunch in our Executive
Suite and everything was formally laid on. Perhaps you will
recall we were to continue the discussion we had started
regarding the publicity campaign for our new fish-based pet
food.

I had gone to the trouble of preparing the information you
asked for and when you failed to appear I telephoned your
office to find out what had happened. We got through to your
number but there was no reply. During the afternooon we
telephoned three times and when we finally did get a response
your receptionist was unable to say where you were. Frankly
I am thoroughly disenchanted but in fairness I feel you
should at least have a chance to explain what happened.

                                        Yours sincerely

                                        K da Costa

                                        Kenneth da Costa
                                        Marketing Manager

Mr T Cheung
AVA Advertising Agency
Wellesley Court
London NW3 5QA

To Mr Cheung   Note of Phone Call

While you were at lunch a Miss Choy phoned. She was supposed
to be coming for an interview on Monday but her mother has
been taken ill. She wants to come on Wednesday instead - same
time. For the next few days she will be at her mother's place.
They are not on the phone but her mother's address is: Flat 16,
Allardyce Court, Egham.   *Janice Smith*

AVA Advertising Agency

INTERNAL MEMORANDUM

To Personal Assistant   From Tim Cheung

                                         15 January 198-

Consultation

The architects have asked for our final decision on the
choice between an open plan office or separate rooms in
the new offices. I prefer open plan but I remember you
saying a few days ago it has its drawbacks. Will you prepare
for me a list of the pros and cons as you see them. I've
also given thought to your suggestion that although this is
my business it might be to my advantage to consult the staff
more. While I am out of the office perhaps you will collate
your ideas on the subject. Again I'd like the pros and cons.
I'd also like to know how you think the consultations
might take place. I appreciate that as the firm grows I
shall have to introduce some formality into my hitherto
haphazard discussions with my staff. But I would like to
know what my options are and what I am letting myself in for.

                                         p.p. Tim Cheung

                                         K. Brown

Extract from Tim Cheung's Diary for next week:

MONDAY Staff meeting for layout of new offices 10.30
            Interview for Secretary's job — Miss Choy 2.30

TUESDAY Phil Beaumont — Architect — 11.30
             Interview for Secretary's job — Miss Stebbings 2.30

WEDNESDAY K. da Costa — lunch at Brentford 12.30

THURSDAY Tom Kerry — here — 10.30
              Paula Preece — lunch

FRIDAY

6.   The Electronic Knitting Machine

George Ascham was born in Bradford, Yorkshire in 1920 and spent
the early years of his working life in a local woollen mill.
During the Second World War he served in the Royal Engineers,
during which time his talents were more fully utilised and he
emerged from the war with the Distinguished Conduct Medal and the
rank of Lieutenant-Colonel. He was obviously unsuited to return to
the mills in his hitherto lowly capacity and was offered a job in
another company - this time as assistant works manager. Having
tasted success, however, he was not satisfied with a minor role
and used his undoubted engineering skills to design an automatic
knitting and weaving machine. He raised sufficient funds to set up
his own company and produced and sold some 80,000 machines between
1955 and 1975, at which time he disposed of 60% of the equity
(voting) stock to Broughton Engineering Ltd, a Lancashire-based
group specialising in the manufacture of textile machinery.
George gave the remaining 40% of the shares in equal parts to his
sons Justin and Roger who were also retained as directors. At that
time the talk was of expanding production and breaking into new
markets. Then came a marked downturn in sales in line with the
world-wide economic recession.

Harry Broughton, Chairman of Broughton Engineering, and his
board of directors responded by closing down the Ascham factory
and disbanding its workforce, much to the chagrin of the Ascham
family. George Ascham saw this as the death of his brainchild
and his sons Justin and Roger lost their livelihoods. The
majority stockholders enforced a voluntary winding up of George
Ascham and Sons Ltd. The real property and plant were disposed of
and the proceeds used to repay the creditors. When all debts had
been paid the receiver was able to distribute 30p to the holders
of each £1 ordinary stock unit.

The winding up of the company was completed eighteen months
ago and since then George has died leaving his £100,000 estate to
his widow, Mandy, for her life and thereafter the remainder to
Justin and Roger in equal shares. The trustees of the estate are
a bank trust corporation and the family solicitor - a Daniel
Harman. Some personal antipathies have developed between the
brothers as a result of the administration of the estate and
relations are now strained between them.

Justin has retained an interest in the old knitting machine
developed by his late father and, aware of the possible applications of the microprocessor, he has persuaded an international
computer company to provide him with a simple but effective program which would update the knitting machine dramatically. With

34

the new device the machine could be programmed to produce a garment without human intervention once the appropriate program had been selected. The programs could be purchased by the user in much the same way as knitting patterns are bought by hand-knitters. In the case of larger or long-sleeved garments it may be necessary to produce a garment in two halves - the new generation machine then being used to speedily join the seams. The attractiveness of the new machine is that it can be left to its own devices during the knitting process, which is greatly speeded up in any case. For example, a standard woollen dress can be turned out in the course of sixty-five minutes - from start to finish - with only three minutes of attention from the user. He calculates that he has spent approximately £5000 of his own money on developing the initial range of 'micro-chip patterns' as he calls them. The computer company have offered to extend the range on the basis of £1000 for each new design and £200 for each cassette containing the program.

Justin has patented the new machine in the UK and is now attempting to patent it internationally. He has spent a further £1000 on fees for a market analysis from a firm of marketing consultants. He envisages holding a library of pattern-cassettes which will then be available for a hiring fee of about £10. The basic knitting machine would cost about £300 and an optional stand for the machine would cost another £50. These figures do not include Value Added Tax. At this moment of time it is calculated that a standard dress could be produced for approximately £30 (including the cassette hiring fee and the cost of the wool).

Justin has been pleased to discover that the old factory is at present on the market at what he regards as a reasonable figure (£100,000 for the freehold - or £50,000 for a 21-year lease at £2000 a year excluding rates). He has calculated that he will need £120,000 to spend on the necessary plant and equipment. With this amount of capital equipment he would expect to produce up to 600 of the new machines a week. He has £30,000 of his own money to invest in the business and is now preparing to ask his bank manager for financial support to get the new project 'off the ground'.

You are asked to play the role of Justin Ascham's personal assistant. He has asked you to let him have a concise report covering two vital aspects of his new project. First, he wants to know what sort of questions his bank manager might ask him when he applies for loan facilities: he wants to be forewarned. He emphasises that there is a vital need for finance if the project is to reach fruition. He asks you to include a break-even chart in your report based on fixed costs of £95,000 per week at every level of production and variable costs at £80 per machine/unit. Stands and cassettes are not included in these calculations.

He sees his interview with the bank manager as of critical importance. But he also wants to know what you think of the project generally. He talks specifically of 'threats and opportunities'. He wants to know your views.

An abridged copy of the marketing consultants' report follows:

```
                    ABRIDGED REPORT
To Justin Ascham Esq.              From Consuma Research Ltd
                                        Northbourne Terrace
                                        Bloomsbury
                                        London, WC2
                                        date (25th ultimo)
```

Product

A fully automated knitting and weaving machine capable of
producing a range of simulated hand-knitted woollen garments
according to attachable/detachable cassettes with human
intervention limited to setting up and seaming. Our contact
has been restricted to an inspection of blueprints and
verbal descriptions, but on the assumption that the machine
is efficient in operation it is superior in design and
performance to anything at present available either in the
UK or elsewhere.

Price

Our research has been conducted on the basis that the basic
machine will be offered at a net price of £300 to £350 and
that the program packages will retail at a price of £300;
or alternatively hired from the manufacturer at a weekly
rental of £10 to £15 including postage (UK only). A specially
designed stand is also to be available at a net price of £50.

Distribution

In the UK distribution will be essentially through the media
of (a) a particular mail order house and (b) selected
department stores. Overseas agents would be used in other
markets, in which case they would hold and hire the library
of program cassettes.

Publicity

In return for a favourable discount the mail order house has
agreed to run a two-page spread extolling the virtues of the
new machine. It has also been agreed that they should
hold and hire a library of program cassettes. The department
stores in five major cities will be used for public demonstrations given by a small team of expert-trained exhibitors.

Market

Markets are sought for an output of 1200-1500 machines per
month. On the evidence of the previous sales levels of the
earlier George Ascham models and our enquiries in the home
market it seems likely that approximately half of these sales
could be achieved in the UK. It follows that substantial
export orders must be obtained and our main effort has been
directed towards potential overseas markets where appropriate
conditions exist and satisfactory agencies are available.
The epitome of our research is shown in the attached schedule.
(see Table 6.1). The estimate of the market share available
to the new Ascham machine is based on three factors, namely
(a) the relative merits and demerits of competing models,
(b) the strength and likely reactions of existing competing
manufacturers and (c) the varying features of the alternative
markets. While it is not suggested that the annual turnover
of knitting machines in the listed countries represents a
peak of the potential market, it indicates the patent demand
for hand-knitting machines, if not the latent demand. We
have centred our research on groups of neighbouring countries,
each group representing a single market, in the sense that
the agencies likely to undertake the business of distributing
the products operate across the respective national boundaries.

Recommendations

Before an appropriate strategy can be adopted it will be
necessary to select the overseas territories which are likely
to be the most fruitful markets. There are no obvious choices
but if you let us know which of the six groups you would most
like us to investigate further we will be happy to make
further proposals.

Vicky da Costa

                    Vicky da Costa

TABLE 6.1

Groups of countries	Population (in millions)	Estimated sales of knitting machines last year (nat. currency in millions)	Price of closest substitute to Ascham machine (in nat. currency)	Estimated market share available to Ascham machine (%)	Main competitor
Group One					
Canada	22.1	$3.95	$635	25	German company which has a 50% share of the market but product is markedly inferior to Ascham's machine
USA	210.4	$21.55	$650	25	
Group Two					
Norway	4.0	4.25 Kr	4500 Kr	40	Swedish company with 35% of the market – but declining: product has not been updated in last 5 years
Sweden	8.1	7.90 Kr	4300 Kr	40	
Finland	4.8	6.86 Mkk	4000 Mkk	75	
Group Three					
Belgium	9.8	68.5 Fr	21500 Fr	20	Main competitor would be same German company as Group One – has 40% of the market share
Netherlands	13.4	20.0 Gld	1600 Gld	30	
Group Four					
Germany	62.0	312.7 DM	1400 DM	10	German company as in Group One – has 75% of the market
Austria	7.5	24.5 Mk	9000 Mk	10	

TABLE 6.1 cont.

Groups of countries	Population (in millions)	Estimated sales of knitting machines last year (nat. currency in millions)	Price of closest substitute to Ascham machine (in nat. currency)	Estimated market share available to Ascham machine (%)	Main competitor
Group Five					
Argentina	24.4	not known	6900 Peso	75	Only machines found were imported from the US (two models) (available but hard to find)
Chile	10.2	not known	none found	75	
Uruguay	3.0	not known	none found	75	
Peru	14.9	not known	none found	75	
Group Six					
France	52.1	376.5 Fr	3500 Fr	10	German company as in Group One has 40% of the market; Swiss company with machine broadly comparable with Ascham's has 30% share
Switzerland	6.4	31.0 Fr	1400 Fr	5	

7. Dateline Lagos

James Adesina has recently returned to Nigeria after completing a
course of business studies and management in London. Before the
course he worked for his Uncle Elijah who was the principal shareholder and chief executive of Ebokpomwen Office Supplies Ltd, a
private company with its head office in Lagos. James had been
financed by his uncle while in England and has now rejoined the
company in the role of personal assistant to him.

In the early days the business was based in Enugu, Elijah's
home town, but as expansion continued premises were also acquired
in Kaduna and the head office was transferred to Lagos. One of the
problems is that of communication since the three branches are at
least 500 kilometres from each other. Ebokpomwen's suppliers are
manufacturers in Britain, the US and Germany. The company do not
process any of the products they sell: they simply distribute
them, supplying any expertise required.

'We've been so busy', Elijah told him. 'There are a number of
things need looking at. I just haven't got round to them yet. Now
you've come back you can have a look into them for me.'

He took James into his office and introduced him to a folder
with 'James Adesina' in bold print across the face of it.

'Here's a collection of items you might look at to start with',
he said. 'Here's a diagram (Figure 7.1) which shows you a break-
down of our sales. You can see we've started selling word processors . . . It means we're having to recruit a different sort
of sales representative. They've got to know what the processors
can do. They've got to know what they're talking about. We've sent
some of our original team on special courses, but when we recruit
now we have to be more careful. You haven't met Francis Wokoma,
our new Personnel Manager. He took over from Nkamanu when he left
us last year. He used to give our sales reps a personality test as
last year. He used to give our sales reps a personality test as
part of the selection procedure. You may have seen it when you
were with us before. Well, Wokoma studied in the US and he's
developed a testing procedure from something he learned over
there. I've always thought our personality test was OK but
Wokoma says it isn't. He's produced these tables to prove it. I
can't make head or tail of them. Perhaps you'd look into it for
me?' (See Table 7.1 and Figures 7.2 and 7.3.)

Elijah Ebokpomwen gave his nephew a few moments to study the
papers before he turned them over and moved on to the next item
in the file.

FIGURE 7.1

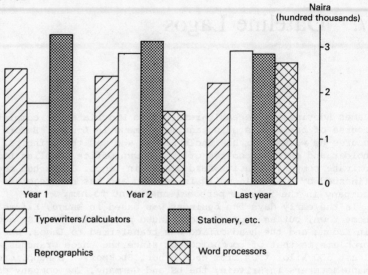

2 naira = £1 approximately

TABLE 7.1   Sales achieved by staff during last year

Salesman's name (branch in brackets)		Personality test score (A = High/ H = Low)	Wokoma's test score (%)	Sales achieved last year (naira)
W. Achebe	(L)	E	69	32,569
T. Aluko	(L)	C	49	27,237
B. Azikwe	(E)	B	36	15,226
I. Bello	(K)	B	60	31,547
L. Ehime	(E)	D	57	26,005
C. Fagunwa	(L)	F	38	20,489
A. Iman	(K)	D	65	34,684
B. Musa	(K)	A	79	38,849
A. Nwankwo	(E)	C	52	22,584
I. Oso	(K)	C	45	18,347
D. Soyinka	(L)	E	42	23,814
M. Wali	(L)	E	41	17,049

Note: Only staff recruited during previous year who took both the Personality Test and Wokoma's Selection Test for sales staff are included in this list.

FIGURE 7.2   Correlation between selection test assessment for salesmen and subsequent performance in terms of sales achieved

(a)   Nkamanu personality test: test invalid - no correlation

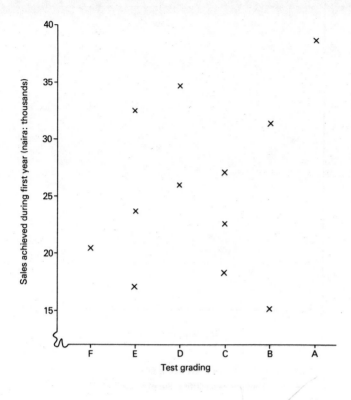

FIGURE 7.2 cont.

(b) Wokoma selection test: test valid - positive correlation

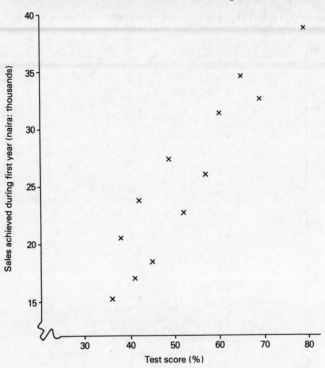

FIGURE 7.3 Test for clerical candidates

Ebokpomwen Office Supplies Ltd

Name...
Post applied for.........................
Column 1 gives the names of some of our customers
Column 2 gives the unpaid amounts outstanding on their accounts
Column 3 gives their credit rating according to the scale

    A   credit allowed up to ₦ 500
    B   credit allowed up to ₦ 1,000
    C   credit allowed up to ₦ 1,500

You are asked to complete column 4 by placing a tick (✓) or a
cross (✗) in the appropriate position to indicate whether or
not the customer's account is within the limits laid down.

Column 1	Column 2 (₦)	Column 3	Column 4
Bisalla J.	324.97	A	
Garba K.	1,125.15	C	
Haruna I.	765.36	C	
Iwegbu K.	35.75	A	
Nobi Stores Ltd	2,578.50	B	
Nwapa F.	887.34	A	
Ochefu A.	998.98	B	
Okiko J.	1,549.00	C	
Olaitan C.	1,500.00	C	
Omotoso I.	400.00	A	
Rotibi L.	663.13	A	
Wali & Son	2,156.70	B	

'He's introduced a test for candidates for clerical jobs too',
he said wryly. 'This is the sort of thing he makes them do before
he employs them. He seems to go to a lot of trouble. I don't see
the point of it, but perhaps you do?' (See Figure 7.3.)

He let James look at the form briefly before turning to the
next paper.

'Here are the latest sales figures we have', Elijah said. 'Results
are patchy - I'd like to know what you think of them. I need to
know what sales we can expect over the next couple of years so
that I can make the necessary plans. What sort of trends do you
see emerging? Perhaps you could produce some moving averages and
let me know what they show?'

TABLE 7.2   Monthly sales over last two years (in naira: thousands)

	Last year				Year before last			
	Lagos	Kaduna	Enugu	Total	Lagos	Kaduna	Enugu	Total
Jan	41.1	38.3	22.8	102.2	37.5	27.7	21.5	86.7
Feb	35.2	36.5	17.6	89.3	32.8	27.9	18.7	79.4
Mar	30.0	38.7	14.2	82.9	32.1	26.5	25.7	84.3
Apr	26.9	29.0	18.9	74.8	22.8	20.3	16.4	59.5
May	28.0	29.8	19.7	77.5	30.9	23.6	16.2	70.7
Jun	41.2	40.5	17.8	99.5	38.0	32.3	18.2	88.5
Jul	50.7	45.5	23.7	119.9	48.9	35.8	20.3	105.0
Aug	44.6	43.3	19.8	107.7	40.4	36.8	21.5	98.7
Sep	33.1	41.7	20.8	95.6	40.7	40.5	17.6	98.8
Oct	39.7	29.6	19.6	88.9	31.5	28.6	18.9	79.0
Nov	44.9	33.5	17.7	96.1	39.2	26.5	25.8	91.5
Dec	43.6	45.8	20.6	110.0	38.5	39.7	20.5	98.7

James was glad to have reached the last item in the file that
had been prepared for him, but his uncle did not let him off the
hook so easily. He continued to explain his problems:

'Francis Wokoma has got some ideas too on how we ought to motivate the salesmen. I've always organised this sort of thing myself. We've got twenty-seven sales representatives in all: seven
at Enugu, six at Kaduna, the rest at head office. We pay them a
good wage and I make sure they put in a good effort. They are
given lists of customers they are to call on. If it's an important customer they're allowed an hour. For smaller customers
they're allocated thirty minutes and so on. They write a brief
report on each visit. I like to know where they are and what
they're doing. I make each of the branch managers keep the
records so I can see them whenever I want to make an inspection.
Wokoma doesn't think it's a good idea. He says we should pay
the sales reps a 5% commission on all sales and he says we
should let them choose who to visit and when - and let them
decide how long to spend with each customer. (He shrugged his
shoulders and grimaced.) Maybe it's a good idea but I don't
want to make any mistakes . . . things are going pretty well
as they are. (He turned back to the latest sales figures.) At
the moment we give our salesmen a price list with the price
they have to quote but Wokoma says we should give our men some

43

discretion. He says we ought to let them quote lower prices - up to 10% lower - to get extra business. He thinks they should be able to do this without referring back to their branch managers. And if there are complaints - if there is any faulty equipment or material he says the reps should be able to use their own discretion, even if it means buying back unwanted stock. He says its called job enrichment. Fine - as long as it works.'

James realised he was going to have to earn his keep even if it was his uncle's firm.

'You can visit the offices and meet our people next week but I'd like your reactions before that. I shall be up at Kaduna for a few days. Let me have a brief report for when I come back. I want to know what you think of Wokoma's ideas. What actions, if any, would you recommend? What sort of problems do you anticipate - on the evidence I've given you of course?'

James realised his uncle was testing him out as well as using him as a managerial aide. He turned back to the file and studied the papers again.

YOUR ASSIGNMENT
Draft a report such as James might have prepared for his new boss. The only other information available to him is shown in Figure 7.4.

FIGURE 7.4   Organisation chart

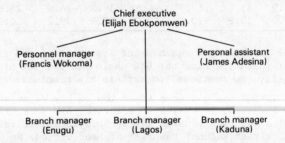

Note: The chief executive assumes the responsibility for purchasing materials and equipment. He also determines sale prices and arranges advertising nationally and locally. There was a crisis recently when a new photocopier was introduced. Large stocks of reprographic material associated with the earlier model thereby became obsolete - at a substantial cost to the firm. The problem was worsened by the fact that supplies of paper for the new machine ran out causing irritation and inconvenience to the customers.

8. Horder and Ziff Pharmaceutics

One of the explanations for the world's population explosion
during the twentieth century has undoubtedly been the increasing
availability and effectiveness of medicines. And that in turn
accounts for the growth of the modern pharmaceutics industry.

For Horder and Ziff Pharmaceutics Plc the story starts in 1897
when Jeremy Horder, the youngest son of a Bristol clergyman, set
himself up as an apothecary in the City of London. As well as
selling his various medications and potions to the City gentlemen
he began to provide them in bulk for others of his profession in
the outlying districts. By the outbreak of war in 1914 he had
switched completely to wholesale operations. It was then that the
business faced its first major crisis, since a large part of its
medical supplies came from Germany. Fortunately for Jeremy his
sister had married an American doctor and when she heard of her
brother's predicament she was able to put him in touch with a
New York merchant, Solomon Zioff, who was able to bridge the gap
in the supplies of vital medications.

Subsequently, Solomon Ziff visited England and after lengthy
discussions with Jeremy they agreed to set up a new company,
Horder and Ziff, based in London but essentially distributing
the products provided by Ziff's firm in New York. The business
expanded steadily through the 1920s and 1930s even after the death
of the founders. At that time the Horder family bought out the
interest of the Ziffs, but in 1961, shortly after the company went
public, it was taken over by an American pharmaceutics group. Re-
named Horder and Ziff Pharmaceutics Ltd (now Plc) the company
operates as a wholly owned subsidiary of the American holding
company.

The company now has four principal divisions:

Pharmaceutical manufacturing. This is the largest of the divisions
in terms of turnover and workforce. It is the division which is
responsible for research and the team of chemists at Horder and
Ziff have achieved some useful breakthroughs, particularly in the
field of veterinary medicine. Production is concentrated on
injectable solutions and since it is a highly competitive market,
substantial sums need to be spent on research to keep ahead of
competitors. The division's resources are supplemented by loans
from the holding company - the hope being that the research team
is on the point of a major breakthrough in the search for a cure
for cancer.

Pharmaceutical distribution. This division is responsible for
providing a distribution network for the group's products. The

customers include wholesalers and hospitals throughout the United Kingdom and Europe. The products are marketed under the brand name of Restora, though the general public would not be familiar with this since the medications tend to be used by dispensers in composite prescriptions or within the hospital wards and operating theatres.

In this highly competitive market the company is concentrating sales in two specialist areas, injectable solutions (42% of total turnover in this division) and dialysis treatments - blood filters (22%). Last year an attempt was made to increase sales by offering substantial discounts on sales to hospitals, but there was a marked absence of a commercial approach by the hospital administrators. There was no additional business and a sharp decline in profitability.

Surgical instruments. High precision instruments for hospital surgery are sold largely through technical catalogues. Supplies are sent from the group's workshops in Baltimore and stored in the London warehouse for onward transmission. There is a small team of specialist staff, trained in the US, who offer an advisory service to the medical profession. The team is run by an American manager with medical qualifications who has been seconded from the parent company.

The instruments are designed and produced for the North American market but have a world-wide reputation in areas such as neuro-surgical, ophthalmic and microsurgery. Although there is intense competition in this market (especially from Germany and Sweden) profit margins remain comparatively high.

Veterinary distribution. This division distributes a fifty/fifty mix of products from the parent corporation and the British company's manufacturing division. The sales are concentrated in the UK (85%) and consist mainly of injector solutions and associated products. Attempts have been made in recent years to break into European markets, spearheaded by some new treatments which were discovered to protect dairy herds against foot and mouth disease. Unfortunately it has not been possible to exploit these clinical advances commercially because competitors have been able to reproduce the treatments without difficulty.

Some notion of the scale of operations in the different divisions can be gleaned from Figure 8.1.

Research

Work is being done on a new drug which promises to help in the war against cancer. A series of experiments are being conducted on animals. In the latest of these a total of thirty-six rhesus monkeys have been injected with a fast-acting carcinogen (cancer-inducing substance). Three of the subjects were left untreated and these died as expected within twenty-one days. The remaining animals were injected on day seven with varying amounts of the new compound solution which is being called 'Delta Nine' at this stage. There are three variants of the drug being tested and while all are proving to have some beneficial effects the researchers have to decide which variant is producing the best results.

On the evidence presented in Table 8.1, which of the three variants would seem to be most effective in delaying the advance of the cancer in the rhesus monkeys?

FIGURE 8.1   Turnover, trading profit and workforce in the various
divisions

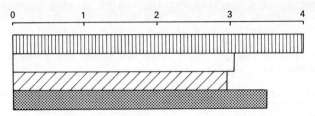

Annual turnover last year (£ million)

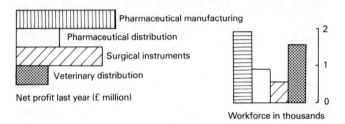

Pharmaceutical manufacturing
Pharmaceutical distribution
Surgical instruments
Veterinary distribution

Net profit last year (£ million)

Workforce in thousands

TABLE 8.1   Days survived after injection of carcinogen

Size of Delta Nine injection	Variant 1	Variant 2	Variant 3
1 ml	22	24	23
2 ml	26	23	20
3 ml	28	27	24
4 ml	29	26	21
5 ml	35	29	23
6 ml	30	30	25
7 ml	29	32	28
8 ml	38	30	23
9 ml	39	34	28
10 ml	41	32	28
11 ml	39	33	30

A lesser research project involved a vaccination procedure to
counter what is known as Q-fever. A news item in the *Guardian* of
6 February 1982 indicated the type of problem which is created by
the virus.

A new outbreak of Q-fever which may have caused the death of
one person, is worrying health officials in South Wales, where
one of the largest recorded outbreaks of the disease occurred
last summer. Q-fever was first identified in Queensland,
Australia, in the 1930s. The disease, which is transmitted by
livestock, was given the initial Q for query . . . About 100
cases of Q-fever are reported in Britain each year. Q-fever is
sometimes carried on infected straw dust blowing in the wind.
The disease, which does not affect animals, very rarely kills
and generally produces symptoms similar to influenza.

47

Again animals have been used by the Horder and Ziff research team. In this case the experimental subjects were rats. The experiments were slightly different from those previously described. First, there was a specific vaccination of varying amounts of the drug being tested. Then, three days later, the subjects were injected with a specific dose of the Q-virus. A second experiment followed and in this case the treatment was given three days after the injection of the Q-virus. Table 8.2 shows the results of these two experiments.

TABLE 8.2   Time taken (in days) for effects of Q-virus to disappear

Dosage of vaccination or treatment (ml)	Vaccination before Q-virus injection	Treatment after Q-virus injection
0.5	27	23
1.0	23	25
1.5	18	27
2.0	15	27
2.5	19	40*
3.0	9	40
3.5	7	37
4.0	6	40*
4.5	9	38
5.0	10	40
5.5	7	39

* the test period ended on day 40 when these rats were still infected.
Note: Of three rats which were injected with the Q-virus and left untreated, one died on day 33, while the other two were still suffering from the disease on day 40.

Group control
Michael Malik is an executive assistant attached to the staff of the vice president in the parent corporation entrusted with responsibility for maintaining control over the numerous subsidiaries in the group. He has just completed a month's stay with Horder and Ziff and he has now drafted a report to his chief covering certain aspects of their operations. The report reads:

ZIFF DRUGS, INC.
NEW YORK

To Robert Ackerman   From Michael Malik
   Vice President   Executive Assistant

Subject: Horder and Ziff (London)   Date

The company operates from premises in central London and acts essentially as a distribution agent for the group though some research and manufacturing is also undertaken. While the company is long established and enjoys substantial contacts with medical institutions, it lacks flexibility in its approach and depends rather heavily on sales to the National Health Service. If one accepts the acid test as growth of business then the weakness of this operation becomes obvious. Allowing for the effects of inflation there has been no growth of sales over the past five years. In the circumstances the decline in profitability experienced in every one of the divisions might easily have been predicted.

Identifying the problem areas:

(1) Operating costs. These have increased considerably - mainly in areas outside the company's control. Costs of petrol, electricity, heating and other items have increased during the past five years and few compensatory economies have been achieved. Even more damaging have been the rise in wages and the outgoings on the property. The new computer which is being installed will no doubt make improvements by speeding up reordering and delivery, and by allowing reductions in the volume of stock held in the stores. But a lack of space generally will remain an inhibiting factor. The most disturbing feature in the situation is that whereas this company was one of the most cost-effective distributors in the group they are now increasingly costly compared with other units.

. (2) Research duplication. While the record of researchers in this company has been outstanding bearing in mind the limited expenditure incurred, much of the work they are doing is being duplicated elsewhere in the group and particularly in the Baltimore laboratories. There appears to be a lack of communication between the two groups of researchers which must add to the costs for the group and also limit the advances which are made. There would be an obvious advantage if the group were to lay down the parameters for the London researchers and insist on a continuous reporting procedure.

(3) Control and co-ordination. There are four distinct divisions in this company and their business is widely different. Some divisions are more efficient than others and there is a tendency for differing divisional performances to be submerged when the company's accounts are produced for the group. In the past a profit target has been set for the company. In four of the past five years that target has not been achieved, and there would be merit in setting more detailed targets, not only for the company but also for the divisions within the company. Much more guidance could be given and control exercised by the group - at one extreme the divisions could be given prescribed targets for capital expenditure being obliged to justify any abnormal items; at the other extreme the staff in London would benefit from the sort of technical instruction manuals which are used by our staff at Baltimore and elsewhere. Procedures in this company tend to be out of line with those in the group generally and a higher degree of standardisation should be imposed.

(4) Communication. Communication links between Baltimore and London are limited to (a) the single American director who serves on both the parent board of directors and the board of Horder and Ziff; and (b) occasional visits to the United States by the Chairman of the London company though these tend to be regarded as social rather than business occasions.

However, the new computer installation with its planned link-up with Baltimore gives considerable scope for a more comprehensive exchange of information. The question to decide now is what sort of information is required most and therefore has a priority in any programme of integration.

Michael Malik

Michael Malik

QUESTIONS TO BE ANSWERED

1. Do you approve of the use of animals in experiments such as those described here? What are the limitations in such experiments? What would be the risks to a company like Horder and Ziff if they sold drugs which had not been fully tested?

2. To what extent do you think a visitor like Michael Malik can hope to find flaws in an organisation such as this pharmaceutical company? What do you think of his report? What are the merits and demerits of his proposals for more centralised

decision-making within the group? What alternatives are there?

3. What sorts of targets might be set by a parent company for its subsidiaries? How do you think targets can be made realistic? How would you expect deviations from the targets to be dealt with by the parent corporation? Distinguish between major and minor deviations - and short- and long-run solutions.

4. How could the divisions of Horder and Ziff be converted into limited companies? What would be the purpose? What benefits would accrue to the American holding corporation? How do you think the new sub-subsidiaries might be controlled?

5. How would you expect the staff in London to react to the various proposals? How do you think they might be persuaded to accept any suggested changes? To what extent do you think the views of the London staff matter?

9. The Office Manager — In Tray

Most of our manufactured goods are made on mass-production lines
and shoes are not generally an exception. So when one thinks of
shoes which are not only hand-made but also specially tailored to
suit every individual's taste and foot shape, one expects to find
prices becoming quite exorbitant. Yet Paula Jones and her friend
Tina Patel have combined the two apparently incompatible notions
of reasonably priced, high-fashion footwear for ladies. Paula was
on her way to obtaining a degree in electronic engineering when
she discovered a simple application of the technique for body
scanning - this time applied to a three-dimensional measurement
of the foot. The device was both ingenious and inexpensive and
after obtaining the necessary patents she set up in business with
her friend, Tina, who was a talented designer of the more exotic
footwear. Their plan was uncomplicated. They would provide a
number of retailers with their Electronic Measuring Devices
(they called them EMDs) at a modest price and offer their customers the opportunity to have shoes specially made to fit each
foot perfectly. A catalogue of designs would be available from
which the customer could choose the sort of 'upper' she had in
mind. The designs ranged from multi-coloured fabric butterflies
to linked metallic rings: the selection was unlimited.

'There's a market for the older ladies too', Paula had observed
from the outset. 'Bunions and corns, deformities generally - we
can make life a lot easier for a lot of people.'

'Of course they'll not want the exotic designs', Tina said,
'but we could still give them attractive footwear.'

Their first problem was getting the financial backing they
needed. They had the choice of going out for a large volume of
business - with the possibility of large profits and the certain
burden of interest and capital repayments - or going for a
smaller-scale operation with fewer complications. They discussed
the choice quite briefly. Neither of them saw themselves ending
up as business tycoons, so they chose a gentle but professional
approach. They set up a limited company, obtained substantial
accommodation (finance) from their bankers, bought a 21-year
lease for a small factory on a local industrial estate, and began
to organise machines and machinists. Even the most likely
businesses need an element of luck and Paula and Tina were
fortunate that a local shoe factory was closing down at about
the same time as they were setting up PJ Footwear Ltd. They were
able to buy second-hand machines fairly cheaply and, even more
to their advantage, they found a pool of skilled labour available.
They commenced operations nine months ago and have already built

up a substantial turnover.

The problems have tended to come on what Paula and Tina describe as the 'commercial' side. The latest problem emerging centres on the role of the office manager who has 'gone sick'. The reports are that he has had a minor heart attack and is likely to be absent for at least three or four weeks. It is the first week in October.

FIGURE 9.1

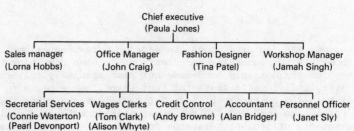

Chief executive
(Paula Jones)

Sales manager (Lorna Hobbs)　Office Manager (John Craig)　Fashion Designer (Tina Patel)　Workshop Manager (Jamah Singh)

Secretarial Services (Connie Waterton) (Pearl Devonport)　Wages Clerks (Tom Clark) (Alison Whyte)　Credit Control (Andy Browne)　Accountant (Alan Bridger)　Personnel Officer (Janet Sly)

YOUR ASSIGNMENT

You are asked to play the role of deputy office manager. Consider the following items on the office manager's desk and decide how to cope with them. Draft any necessary correspondence.

The organisation structure as related to the office manager's job is set out in Figure 9.1. There are 98 employees in all.

JAYS
(Leather) Ltd

Strummer Row
Coventry CV2 B92

Tel:0203 717

date as postmark

The Manager
PJ Footwear Ltd
Cronhelm Drive
Winterton

Ref NJ/KKL

Dear Sir or Madam,

I regret to have to inform you that this company has run into financial difficulties as a result of the action of our bankers in calling in an outstanding loan. It is the directors' hope that we shall be able to meet some of our commitments but we cannot give precise details at this stage. In the circumstances we are calling a meeting of creditors under Section 278 of the Companies Act 1948 and write to advise you that this will take place at these offices at 3.00 p.m. on the 28th of next month.

I hope to be able to provide you with more information when the creditors meet.

Yours sincerely,

Norman Jay
Managing Director

PS The amount of your account outstanding is £195.75

PJ Footwear Ltd

MEMORANDUM

To John Craig   From Lorna Hobbs

I've prepared some material for the Evening Post and I
wonder if you'd look at it for me, John, before I send
it off. Paula would normally approve it but she's on
holiday until the 14th and the proofs have got to go in
by Friday. Any comments would be appreciated. Incidentally,
Connie Waterton seems to be giving that new girl Pearl a
rough ride. I've been into your office a few times lately
and there seems to be a real clash of personalities. A
shame because she seems a pleasant young lady. Much better
than her predecessor. At least she's polite and helpful.

Lorna

1 November 108-

WOULD YOU LIKE TO WEAR SHOES
THAT WERE MADE JUST FOR *YOU*
AND NO ONE ELSE? COME AND SEE
OUR SENSATIONAL THREE-
DIMENSIONAL ELECTRONIC FOOT
SCANNER. HAVE A LOOK AT SOME OF OUR FANTASTIC
SHOE DESIGNS AT THE SAME TIME.

Space here for a couple of Tina's new designs - as eye-catching as possible

Your shoes will be ready within 14-21 days of ordering.
Demonstrations are available at any of the following stores in
Winterton:
    Fredericks, Market Square
    Johnson & Winterbourne, High Street
    Louella's Shoe Fayre, Granada Street
    Sandy's Shoe Boutique, St James Square

Charles Barker
Fashion Shoes

Shelleys Walk
Bradford BD1 1BR

Tel: 0274 312

date as postmark

PJ Footwear Ltd
Cronhelm Drive
Winterton

Ref.EJS/PMB

Dear Sirs,

Over the past three months we have ordered a total of 132
pairs of your High Fashion shoes and have been concerned to
note the increasing time it is taking between giving the
order and receiving delivery of the shoes. We have carefully
monitored the times because a number of our customers have
complained at the delays and we have been pressured by phone
calls, letters and visits from people waiting for shoes they
have ordered.

We have found that the average time taken is between five
and six weeks although in your original advertising material
you made great play on the fact that all orders could be
effected within two to three weeks at the most. Of course we
attempt to placate our customers but they are often wanting
the shoes for special occasions, holidays, etc., and we find
ourselves under fire for reasons we cannot explain. From our
point of view the matter is very serious and we are considering
whether to discontinue this line unless we can be assured of
a better service to our customers in future.

We would like to hear from you.

Yours sincerely,

C Small

Manager

PJ Footwear Ltd
MEMORANDUM

To Mr Craig   From Mrs C Waterton
   Office Manager

During your absence last week I had two spots of bother with
Pearl Devonport. I am putting it on record because I feel
very annoyed at what has happened and I do not intend to be
held responsible for the consequences. First, as you know
Pearl and I are responsible for manning the switchboard
during the lunch hour. Pearl has been taking the first hour
from noon to one o'clock. Each day I have had to wait for up
to twenty minutes for her and I am not going to do this any
longer. She just does not take any notice of what I tell her
and it did not make any difference when you spoke to her.
She came back to the office grinning all over her face.

She has been at least twenty minutes late every morning this
week and I feel resentful that I make such a big effort to
get into work on time and she gets away with it so easily.

Frankly it is a case of either she goes or I do.

C Waterton (Mrs)

29 September 198-

GK Ltd

KERRINGTON WORKS
DERBY

Telephone (0332) 74

3 October 198-

Dear Sir,

Reference Account No.3563/7

We note that your account with us, standing at £956.75,
remains unsettled though the machinery was delivered in late
July. We would like to remind you that we have recently
introduced a cash discount of 3 per cent which is deducted
on all bills paid within three months. You would still qualify
for this discount if you paid your account within the next
21 days.

Yours faithfully,

Janet Crisp

pp Credit Controller

The Office Manager,
PJ Footwear Ltd,
Cronhelm Drive,
Winterton

PJ Footwear Ltd
MEMORANDUM

To Mr J Craig   From Jamah Singh

You asked for details of the orders we have dealt with over
the past six weeks. I have collected the following data for
you.

Conventional shoe sizes	High fashion range	Standard range
$3\frac{1}{2}$	37	11
4	83	31
$4\frac{1}{2}$	112	78
5	203	99
$5\frac{1}{2}$	434	113
6	696	108
$6\frac{1}{2}$	787	80
7	303	13
$7\frac{1}{2}$	38	1

I understand you were going to analyse the figures for me
and draw some general conclusions which might be helpful if
we introduce mass production lines at a later stage.

30 September 198-

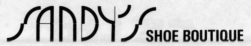

SANDY'S SHOE BOUTIQUE

St James Square
Winterton

30th September 198-

Dear Sirs,
        I have received your letter asking for payment of the
outstanding account for the High Fashion shoes. Incidentally,
the account was for £185.75 <u>not</u> £186.75 as your invoice shows.
When your Mr Marsh came to see me last August he told me that
I would have a chance to collect the money from my customers
before you called for payment. The problem is that you took
so long to send the orders through I lost contact with two of
my clients so I now have shoes on my hands which I am most
unlikely to sell.
        I have tried to phone your office in the lunch hour -
which is the only time I can use the phone - but I have been
unable to get a reply from your number though the phone is
ringing. I would have explained the situation earlier if I
had been able to get through. I have another six pairs of
shoes on order (£200 approximately in value) and I can only
hope you will not let me down on delivery for these.
        I do not see how you can expect me to pay for the shoes
until I have sold them. I have put two pairs of unwanted
shoes on general display and no doubt someone will buy them
in due course. Then I will settle the account.

                                        Yours faithfully,

                                        Sandy Matlock

                                        Sandy Matlock

PJ.Footwear Ltd
Cronhelm Drive
Winterton

PJ Footwear Ltd

MEMORANDUM

To John   From Paula

Sorry you were unwell yesterday.Hope you are better now.I
was very interested in our discussion at lunch on Tuesday.
I am going on holiday now but I would appreciate it if you
could put down your ideas in writing for when I get back.

I want to know particularly how you suggest we might grade
different jobs in the organisation — I think you said we
ought to do some job evaluation.There is no doubt we are
coming up against all sorts of administrative problems as
we expand and we've obviously got to organise ourselves.
You are the expert! But please be brief and do not make it
a long report.I just want an outline of what you've got in
mind at this stage so that I can decide what to do next.
See you in a fortnight!

                                        Paula

                                        29 September 198-

10. The Board Meeting — Group Role Play

The directors of the Oracle Group of companies are having their
weekly board meeting at their headquarters in London. The Chairman
of the holding company, Frank McKellan, will shortly be facing the
shareholders at the Annual General Meeting and wishes to clear up
a number of outstanding matters before that time. The agenda
includes the following items and you are invited to work through
these, playing the role of the directors at the meeting. Consider
the various implications and reach decisions such as might be
made by the board - on the evidence provided here. Use normal
boardroom procedures as far as possible. Resolutions should be
formally proposed and seconded. There should be adequate discussion
under the control of the Chairman and then a vote should be taken
(each director being entitled to one vote with the Chairman having
the casting vote). One member of the group should play the role of
the company secretary and record the resolutions and the decisions
reached by the board.

The Agenda
1. Consideration of a request received from the chief executive of
    ABC Newsagents Ltd to be given a 25% discount on list price,
    instead of the present 12½% for supplies purchased from
    Cardex Ltd. Net purchases from Cardex amounted to £108,000
    during the past nine months (see Figure 10.1 and Table 10.1
    for group structure).
2. It having been agreed at the last board meeting that Borealis
    Publications Ltd should grant a loan of £250,000 to Candida
    Confections Ltd for a term of five years, it is now necessary
    to consider the rate of interest to be charged on this loan.
3. Choice of board's candidate for a director to replace Alan
    Dolby who is retiring through ill health from the board of
    the subsidiary, Cardex Ltd, next month (see Appendix 10.1 for
    existing directors and a list of candidates now under con-
    sideration).
4. It having been the custom to reward long-service directors on
    their retirement, consideration is now to be given to a
    possible gratuity to Alan Dolby on his retirement from the
    board of Cardex (see Appendix 10.2 for details of his career
    and past gratuities paid to retiring directors).
5. It having been the custom to donate a sum of £20,000 to
    Conservative Party funds in each of the four previous years,
    it is now necessary to consider the question of this year's
    donation.

6. Consideration of the Group Personnel Director's Report on the proposed development of a new European newspaper - *The European Oracle* (see Appendix 10.3).

TABLE 10.1

Company	Main business activity	Equity owners (percentage of votes)		Net assets (£ million)	Net profit (per annum) (£ million)
The Oracle (Holding) Co. Ltd	No trading	F. McKellan (Chairman) W. McKellan* Others	43 8 49	129.7	28.5
Thomas and Parsons Ltd	Paper manufacture and packaging	Oracle (Holding) Co. Ltd	100	34.0	7.5
The Daily Oracle (News) Ltd	National daily newspaper	Oracle (Holding) Co. Ltd	100	95.3	1.9
Borealis Publications Ltd	Childrens and specialist magazines - Panda comics, Property Mart, etc.	Oracle (Holding) Co. Ltd W. McKellan* Centura Pension Fund Others	35 8 38 19	13.5	1.8
Candida Confections Ltd	Sweets and chocolates for children	Oracle (Holding) Co. Ltd Thomas and Parsons Ltd Others	18 43 39	2.2	0.5
Cardex Ltd	Greetings cards	Borealis Publications Ltd W. McKellan* W. Hardiman Others	55 15 12 18	9.8	2.7
ABC Newsagents Ltd	Retail newsagents, tobacconists and confectioners	Thomas and Parsons Ltd Others	33 67	29.5	1.5

* W. McKellan (Frank's brother) is a non-executive director in each of these companies.

58

FIGURE 10.1

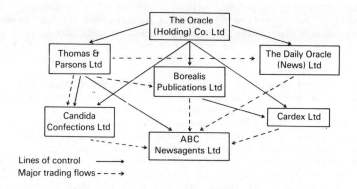

Lines of control ⟶
Major trading flows - - - →

Appendix 10.1

Details of existing directors on the board of Cardex Ltd

BILL HARDIMAN   Chairman/Managing Director, aged 63. Co-founder
of company twenty-three years ago; retained a stake and his
managerial role when the Oracle Group took over in 1975.
W. McKELLAN   aged 62. No departmental responsibilities – is also
on the boards of the holding company and Borealis Publications
Ltd; is a Chartered Accountant.
LAURIE HARDIMAN   Son of Chairman, aged 38. Main interest is in
production; functions as Production Director.
COLIN BREVITT   aged 60. Joined Cardex from Borealis nine years
ago; regarded as the group's expert in artwork.
ALAN DOLBY   aged 66. Now retiring through ill health (see
Appendix 10.2).

List of candidates for directorship on retirement of Alan Dolby

SIR ALEC BRUNDAGE   aged 58. Also a director of a national
supermarket chain, a firm of merchant bankers and the ABC News-
agents. He and his family have substantial shareholdings in
ABC - the exact details are not known but they are believed to
be in excess of 20% of the total equity. It is anticipated that
he would be able to persuade the supermarket to introduce the
Cardex range of greetings cards throughout their 1500 retail
outlets, thus halting a decline in Cardex's share of the market
from 22% to 18% over the past eighteen months.

JULIE MORRISON   aged 32. Business Studies graduate who joined
the *Daily Oracle* after leaving Liverpool Polytech; a special
features editor for 4-5 years then took over senior post in
Cardex; presently Manager of Creative Designs Department having
displayed exceptional talent in designing all sorts of greetings
cards - responsible for seven out of ten of the top-selling new
cards including, 'I'm sorry . . .!' and 'I'd love to hear from
you . . .!', which are now the two best all-year-round selling
lines. Her husband is a computer programmer. There are no
children.

TOM GREENAWAY   aged 48. Has been with Cardex for past twenty-
three years; starting as a sales representative he progressed to
Area Manager and has been Marketing Manager for the past eleven
years. It is known that a competing company in greetings cards -
the market leader in fact - has offered him a senior post in
their organisation. He has just returned from a tour of Canada
and the US with a small sales team, attempting to promote Cardex
in these hitherto untapped markets (only 5% of total sales are
overseas at this stage). One problem which would emerge if
he was elevated to the board would be his replacement as Marketing
Manager. He has lost three Assistant Managers over the last two
years - two left the company, one retired through ill health.
His current Assistant Manager took over two months ago and it is
too soon to know how effective he is going to be.

NICHOLAS O'HARA   aged 45. Senior partner in a London market
research agency with branches in Paris, Bonn and Rome. He has
recently joined the board of The Daily Oracle (News) Ltd. Apart
from his expertise in market research he is a skilled linguist
being able to speak French, German and Spanish fluently. Of the
five partners in his firm two are German nationals and one is
French.

SHEHU MUSA   aged 33. A Nigerian who spends most of his time in
London as Chief Buyer for his family's business. Musa's Stores
sell a wide variety of products - wholesale and retail -
throughout Kano and Kaduna States. They have intimated a
willingness to distribute a number of the group's products

through their company. Production would need to be modified but it is anticipated that this would be a lucrative market for children's comics and greetings cards. Cardex's total exports could be doubled if these Nigerian contacts were established.

Notes
1. Both the Chairman of the group and the Cardex Chairman have interviewed the potential directors. Both would approve of the election of any of them to the Cardex board.
2. The Articles of Association of Cardex Ltd require that a director must hold a minimum of 5000 ordinary shares and these will be made available to any of the above who are proposed as directors to a General Meeting of the shareholders.

Appendix 10.2

ALAN DOLBY
Joined Cardex when company was first formed: started as a foreman in the printing works; became Production Manager in 1972; elected to the board of Cardex in 1975 assuming responsibility for the personnel function (Personnel Director). Mr Dolby suffered a heart attack last year but agreed to remain on the board until a new Personnel Manager could be appointed. This has been done (Mrs E. Charlesworth).

The emoluments paid to Mr Dolby since January 1980 have averaged £28,500 per annum. He will now receive a fixed pension of £10,250 per annum from the contributory pension scheme run by the company. Gratuities paid to previous Cardex directors on retirement:

Name	Years of service on board	Role	Year of retirement	Gratuity
Jack Frayn	5	Non-executive	1975	£5,500
Harry Butt	6	Personnel Director	1975	£15,000
Duncan Caudell	1	Financial Director	1980	£35,000
Alex Courtney	9	Non-executive	1982	£20,000

Appendix 10.3

To Mr Frank McKellan, Chairman

From Ray Teague

Oracle (Holding) Co.Ltd   Group Personnel Director

CONFIDENTIAL   (yesterday's date)

The European Oracle

As requested by the Board of Directors at the last meeting I
visited the offices of the Daily Oracle to discuss with
senior staff some of the implications with regard to the
staffing of a new European daily newspaper for circulation in
the countries of the European Economic Community. My main
consultations were with the Editor, John Strevens, a group of
sub-editors and the company's Personnel Manager (Matthew
Corfield). John Strevens was already aware of the ideas being
floated for the new publication. They seemed generally impressed
with the suggestion to use the new KB12 equipment for the
instantaneous translation of news items in French, German
and Italian fed into various terminals throughout Europe.

   The Oracle team found no flaws with the proposals technically
but they envisaged degrees of resistance from the workforce.
Mr Corfield's views were obviously pertinent in this respect.
He felt the unions would need to be reassured that the new
publication would increase the workload for the London staff.
He felt they would object to the newspapers being printed out
of England — as a matter of principle — and this would probably
be used as a bargaining counter in any new wage agreements.
However it was accepted that our own strategy could be to
emphasise that one of our options was to produce the paper in
France or Germany and use London as a printing and distribution
point.

   A detailed manpower plan is being prepared by Mr Corfield
but at this stage it appears that the Oracle's workforce would
need to be increased by approximately 10% to cope with the
additional volume of work. The major issue with the unions is
likely to be the unavoidable redundancy of certain categories
of workers if the KB12 equipment is introduced. Although only
380 jobs are at stake — out of a total workforce of 3250 —
retraining programmes are virtually impossible because the new
equipment will require staff with lesser skills and lower pay.
We are looking for a high proportion of female staff to operate
the new equipment.

   As the discussions proceeded it was obvious that some of the
sub-editors were increasingly lukewarm about the proposals
One of them asked how many non-British journalists would be
employed. Another commented,'I suppose the management have got
the same counter-strategy for us. If we don't co-operate the
Oracle will be taken over by the French and the Germans.' Many
of the objections they raised after that seemed trifling and
pointless bearing in mind that it had been pointed out to them
that we were only in the exploratory stages of the project.

   It seems that we may well have more to contend with than
unions and shop stewards.

62

11.   The Embassy Court Hotel

Bournemouth as a resort is famed for its equable climate and
its many chines - deep, narrow, pine-clad ravines leading down to
the six miles of sandy beaches. Nestling at the top of one
such picturesque chine is the Northcliffe Hotel. It is one of
the smaller hotels in the area with just 32 bedrooms. Bathrooms
and toilets are provided on each of the three floor levels. The
hotel is not luxurious by any means but there is a friendly
'family' atmosphere largely as the result of the efforts of
Terry and Ann Colborne, the proprietors. The hotel is clean and
efficient. Their eldest son, Jason, has taken over the role
of chef since he acquired a National Diploma in Catering last
summer. Until that point of time the meals tended to be mediocre
but Jason is obviously quite talented and certainly enthusiastic.

   The Colbornes enjoyed a stroke of fortune last year when
they were approached by a major London banking house who were
seeking accommodation for thirty of their staff who were coming
to Bournemouth for a full-time banking course at the local
technical college. As a result the average occupancy level of
the rooms over a full year rose from 35% to approximately 70%
(there are 20 double rooms and 12 singles). The inflow of cash
has coincided with a neighbouring hotel coming onto the market.
Although the Embassy Court is on the adjoining site, it is a very
different hotel from the Northcliffe. It is not only much larger
(it has 86 double bedrooms and 20 singles), but is generally
newer and much more luxurious. All rooms have private bathroom,
colour television, radio and telephone. There are ample car-
parking facilities and easy access to the beach. The owners are
a private limited company and the hotel is run by a manager with
a full-time staff of ten, supplemented by a staff of seven to
twenty temporary and part-time workers in the main holiday
season. The occupancy level of their rooms has varied between
30% and 55% over the past four years, but last year was a
particularly bad one for the hotel (33%) and this no doubt
explains why it is on the market at the present time. The asking
price is £200,000 though the agents handling the sale have hinted
that the owners might be prepared to accept an offer 10% below
that figure. Terry is seriously considering making an offer for
the Embassy Court although he admits the hotel accounts which
have been shown to him are not very impressive. The net profits
over the past four years have averaged £20,000 with a tendency
to fall over the past two years.

   'The trouble is the staff basically', explains the agent. 'The
managing director has been out of the country for some while and

he has had to leave it in the hands of a manager. The manager has been with the hotel for fifteen years but he doesn't seem to be very dynamic. The chef is excellent though. I've had a few meals there myself. I think he's the only one of the staff who would be worth keeping on.'

Ann is perturbed when she hears that the company which owns the Embassy Court is not offering the freehold. They are asking £200,00 for a 99-year lease and there is a proposed ground rent of £1000 per annum to be paid by the leaseholder. But Terry has been in contact with the principal shareholder, a Miss Trehearne, through her solicitor. She owns 60% of the ordinary shares in Embassy Court Hotel Ltd and her solicitor has intimated that she would be prepared to sell her £1 shares for £1.75 each. It appears that Miss Trehearne is an elderly lady who is now living in a rest home. She is being advised by her solicitor. Terry has been given a set of accounts up to the end of December last (see Table 11.1) and he has confidence that the figures give a true and fair view of the financial situation at the Embassy Court.

Ann's father, Brian Shaw, is a retired bank manager and a widower. He has offered to help them finance the project, having great affection for Ann who is his only child. On retirement he came to live near his daughter and her family. In indifferent health, he has laid his cards on the table for them and disclosed the extent of his personal possessions. Apart from his bank pension of £300 a month (after tax) and his old-age pension, he has:

1. The freehold two-bedroomed bungalow 'Dunroamin', Netherbury, Dorset (purchase price in 1975 £32,500)
2. £2500 in Michelin Tyre Company 6¾% Debenture Stock 84/89
3. 3000 Imperial Chemical Industries ordinary stock units of £1 each
4. £15,000 in 3% British Transport stock 1978/88
5. £15,000 in 3½% War Loan
6. 3000 Sungei Bahru Rubber Estates ordinary stock units of 10p each
7. 2000 Crescent Japan Investment Trust ordinary stock units of 50p each
8. Balance on Lloyds Bank Ltd current account £300-£500.

Mr Shaw has told Terry and Ann, 'I'll do anything I can to help you financially. Just let me know what you need. I've got an open mind though obviously I have to protect myself as much as I can.'

This offer of support is obviously invaluable to Terry because he is going to need a lot of capital if he goes ahead with the purchase of the Embassy Court - whether it is by buying the shares from Miss Trehearne or buying the property through the agents. One of his immediate problems is in sorting out his own accounts for the Northcliffe Hotel. He felt that his accountant overcharged him last year for the preparation of the annual accounts and so he is trying to prepare them on his own this time.

He has the previous set of accounts to guide him (see Table 11.2).

TABLE 11.1 Profit and loss account for year ending 31 December 198-: Embassy Court Hotel Ltd

	(£)		(£)
Wages and salaries	117,548	Accommodation receipts	114,689
Victuals	30,734	Restaurant receipts	66,389
Wines and spirits	8,089	Bar takings	24,357
Lighting and heating	1,521		
Repairs and replacements	1,657		
Rates	1,875		
Advertising	305		
Tax	3,106		
Other expenses	1,484		
Directors' emoluments	18,000		
Net profit c/d	21,116		
	205,435		205,435
Dividends	18,000	Net profit b/d	21,116
Transfer to reserve	3,000	Balance b/d	303
Balance c/d	419		
	21,419		21,419

Balance sheet as at 31 December 198-

		(£)			(£)
Ordinary shares of £1 each		150,000	*Fixed assets*		
			Freehold premises		200,000
8% Cumulative preference shares of £1 each		50,000	Furniture and equipment less depreciation		34,563
Reserves		36,000	China and cutlery less depreciation		2,907
Current liabilities					237,470
Creditors	5,481		*Current assets*		
Accrued expenses	209		Stocks-victuals	489	
Appropriation a/c	419		Wines and spirits	986	
		6,109	Debtors	401	
			Cash at bank	2,763	
					4,639
		242,109			242,109

TABLE 11.2   Northcliffe Hotel: Profit and Loss Account for year
ending 31 December 198-

		(£)
Hotel receipts		
Cash	13,322	
Cheques	32,665	45,987
Bar profits		674
		46,661
less Wages for casual workers	1,856	
Salaries - T. Colborne	10,000	
A. Colborne	2,000	
	13,856	
Expenditure on food and drink	14,884	
Entertainment	105	
Lighting and heating	1,705	
Rates (levied by local authority)	3,263	
Advertising	68	
Repairs and replacements	1,974	
Depreciation of furniture and fittings	901	
Bad debts	340	
Decoration - internal	1,900	
external	1,350	
	3,250	
Interest on bank loan	4,250	
		44,596
Net profit to capital a/c		£ 2,065

Balance-sheet as at 31 December

	(£)		(£)
Capital	41,173	Cash at bank	2,285
Add profit for year	2,065	Stocks of food and drinks	377
	43,238	Kitchen equipment and tableware	1,551
Less drawings	2,100	Furniture and bed linen	3,225
	41,138		
		Prepaid accounts	331
Creditors			
Builder/decorator	3,250	Freehold premises	
Others	187	(at cost 1975)	89,250
Bank loan	49,855		
Accrued interest	2,589		
	£97,019		£97,019

Terry has collected as much other information as possible to help him draft the accounts for the year to 31 December last. The details available include:

		(£)
Cheques paid during the year to suppliers of		
food and drinks		22,559
to suppliers of wines and spirits		3,867
Other cheques paid:		
Southern Electricity	1,497	
Southern Gas Board	883	
Builders/decorators	3,250	
T. Colborne (salary)	12,000	
A. Colborne (salary)	2,000	
J. Colborne (salary)	3,605	
T. Colborne (drawings)	2,500	
Local Authority (rates)		
(one quarter in advance)	3,680	
Prestige Advertising	105	
	-------	29,520

Receipts are available for:		
Casual wages paid	3,840	
Bed linen	185	
New furniture	86	4,111

Reference to the bank account shows:	
Cheques paid in from Lloyds	
Bank (for student hostelling)	58,045
Cheques collected from other guests	35,166
Cash from guests paid in	14,805
Bar receipts	4,786
Interest on loan for year	3,663
Balance on current account at 31 December	7,501
Balance of loan account (ditto)	nil

Other information
(1) Two guests left the hotel in August without paying their bills. The bills totalled £355.
(2) Inventories were taken at the end of the year. Food and drink in store was valued at cost £507. Kitchen equipment and tableware was valued for insurance purposes (replacement cost) at £3000. A similar valuation for furniture and bed linen produced a figure of £3500. But the proprietors calculate that they would get only about one-third of these valuations if the goods went to auction.
(3) There are two bills outstanding: the first for wines and spirits (£112); the second for taxes (£568).

YOUR ASSIGNMENT
1. What profit do you calculate the Northcliffe Hotel to have made last year? Produce a set of final accounts for the year.
2. If you were advising the proprietors, on the evidence of these accounts, what warnings would you give?
3. On the evidence available what do you think would be a fair price for the Embassy Court Hotel? What advice would you give

to Terry if he is interested in taking it over? How do you think he might acquire the resources to make a purchase?

4. How do you think Brian Shaw might help his daughter and her husband with minimum risk to himself? What advice would you offer him?

5. What economies would you expect to be achieved if the two hotels were under the same management? Be specific and make as complete a list as possible.

6. Assume the Colbornes take over the Embassy Court, how do you think the hotels should be organised? What specific problems would you envisage if the Embassy Court Hotel Ltd continued to function in its present form? Would it be possible to organise it so that a new company is formed to take over both hotels? What do you see as the least problematical of the alternative structures?

7. If a new company is formed what sort of capital structure would you advise — from Terry Colborne's point of view?

8. What staff problems would you foresee if the Colbornes took over the Embassy Court? What difficulties would you expect them to encounter if they wanted to dismiss any of the present staff?

9. The occupancy rates in both hotels seem very low. How do you think more guests could be encouraged? Consider and evaluate a range of alternatives. Distinguish between short-term and long-term solutions.

10. Assuming that the Colbornes will be seeking some form of loan from their bank manager, draw up a detailed scheme such as Terry Colborne might present to him when making the application.

12.   The Purbeck Holiday Campus

This camp is one of many owned by South Coast Holidays Ltd. It
was acquired by them in 1970 and for many years it operated at a
loss. The directors tried a wide range of ploys in an effort to
make the camp more successful. In turn they raised prices to
make it more exclusive, lowered the prices together with the tone
(going downmarket), advertised extensively and introduced a
succession of camp managers. Finally, the board decided to
dispose of their 'white elephant'. A rival company had even got
round to the point of making an offer for the site when fate took
a hand. The Chairman of the company, Mark Scrivens, was an
active Rotarian in neighbouring Bournemouth and during a function
arranged for overseas students visiting the town, he discovered
some interesting facts. The visitors were generally pleased with
their courses but they had mixed feelings about their
accommodation. They were living *en famille* or in bedsitters and
most agreed that this was the least satisfactory aspect of
their 'learning package'. They gave the company Chairman food
for thought.

Shortly after this experience Mark Scrivens was offering his
fellow directors a way round the problem.

'One of this country's most valuable resources is the
English language', he told his fellow directors. 'Students are
coming to England from all over the world to improve their English.
We've got accommodation we can't sell for eight months of the
year. I am suggesting that we might use our Purbeck camp to cater
specifically for students, providing them with tuition, courses
and libraries, etc. Gentlemen, I'm proposing we develop a college
campus on our Purbeck site - bring in the tutors and offer
students from all over the world an education in an idyllic
setting!'

His colleagues were astonished at his proposals, but Mark
Scrivens was able to convince them that there was a reasonable
prospect of success. Any lingering doubts in the minds of
his fellow directors were dispelled when he produced:

(1) details of the trifling offer which had been made for the
    site by the rival company;
(2) the illustrated brochure he had prepared indicating how the
    campus and courses would be marketed;
(3) the plan for converting the site/buildings for student use
    for an expenditure of £200,000 which they regarded as
    reasonable;
(4) a list of the academics who had offered their services
    full-time or part-time.

FIGURE 12.1   Plan of the Purbeck Holiday Campus

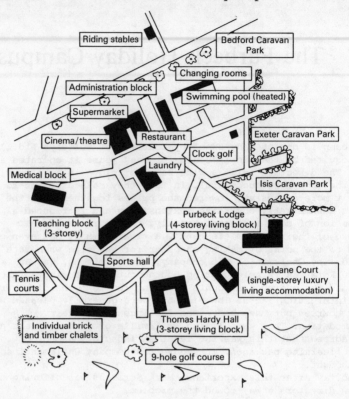

So the student campus in the Purbeck Hills was founded and the board of directors are now assessing the results after the first full year of operation. See Table 12.1 for the statistics that are available to them at this stage.

TABLE 12.1 Comparison of occupancy rates (%) before and after conversion to student campus

| Accommodation | Maximum no. of beds/ berths | Average occupancy rate in each quarter | | | | | | | | Tariff index* |
| | | before conversion | | | | after conversion | | | | |
		1st	2nd	3rd**	4th	1st	2nd	3rd	4th	
Purbeck Lodge	412	5	35	83	8	41	47	69	61	105
Haldane Court	80	10	46	85	12	35	46	53	60	165
T. Hardy Hall	484	5	49	91	15	40	40	40	41	100
Chalets	75	4	32	82	11	53	57	59	39	115
Bedford park	100	0	9	75	12	0	0	0	0	90
Exeter park	120	0	0	72	3	0	0	0	0	85
Isis park	80	8	14	67	12	25	29	40	28	95

* This is an indicator of the charges made per bed/berth, so if the 'standard charge' fixed by management for a bed/berth is £120 per week in the coming year, the charge for a bed in Purbeck Lodge is £120 x 1.05 = £126.
** The Tariff Index in this quarter (July-September) enhanced by 50% to cope with the increased demand during these months. This enhancement has now been removed.
The residential caravans on these parks were disposed of for a total of £35,000.

The two sets of figures in Table 12.1 are broadly comparable because the pricing policy has been to keep the charges for food and accommodation separate from the academic fees. The decision was also taken to keep tuition fees at a minimum so that they simply covered costs under the following headings:

(a) salaries of academic and administrative staff
(b) teaching material and video equipment
(c) text books for library and individual use
(d) educational trips
(e) visiting lecturers' fees (a number of the courses are business or management orientated).

The board feels the results are encouraging bearing in mind that many of the courses on which students are enrolled are of two years' duration. However there have been two untoward occurrences which have somewhat marred the results.

The Fire

In August last year there was a fire in the Sports Hall during the reconstruction work. The building was badly damaged but the company had insured against the possibility of such an occurrence. The board had calculated the extent of their loss in the sum of £25,000 so they were understandably disappointed when they received the following letter from their insurers, three months after the fire.

Grenadier Fire Insurance

Bathgate

Scotland

date as postmark

Dear Sirs,

Claims Department Reference 76/A3547/F

We have now received our Assessor's report covering the fire damage at the Purbeck Campus (to the building described as the Sports Hall) on the night of 23 August last. The delay has largely stemmed from the fact that the building was undergoing certain structural changes at the time of the fire. This office was not informed of these changes and it has been **difficult** for our Assessor to make appropriate valuations. Now these problems have been overcome and we hope we can deal expeditiously with your claim.

There are two essential factors which proscribe your claim, according to our Assessor. First, he estimates that the building in its original state would have been fairly valued at around £60,000 (the value of the land being ignored). He points out that your own valuation of the building was £40,000 as evidenced by the premiums and cover ascribed to these specific buildings. This is to say, in view of the 'subject to average' clause included in the insurance contract, your cover was limited to two-thirds of the building's value. He also estimates that it would cost approximately £21,000 to put the buildings back into their original state and on these grounds compensation could not exceed £14,000, i.e. two-thirds of the damage sustained.

Second, and most disturbingly, the Assessor reports that the fire was believed to be caused when a lighted cigarette end was thrown onto a pile of waste which included items over which petrol had been spilled. On questioning the Site Manager our Assessor discovered that it had been common practice during the programme of converting the building for student use, to store substantial amounts of fuel for use by trucks and cement mixers. In our Assessor's view this greatly increased the fire risk and we would not have been prepared to cover this risk if we had known the circumstances.

We appreciate that your company conducts much business through this office and for this reason we are prepared to make an ex gratia payment, without prejudice, in the sum of £7000 providing this sum is formally accepted within the next twenty-one days in full and complete satisfaction of your claim.

We would earnestly ask you to review the current insurance cover on all the properties in your portfolios to make sure that **none of the properties are under-insured. You might also consider** the advisability of paying additional premiums to cover loss of earnings while a building is being rebuilt after sustaining serious damage.

Yours sincerely,

J Aherne
Manager

The Financial Director
South Coast Holidays Ltd
Salisbury
Wiltshire

The Bankruptcy

The financial director was delighted to find a buyer for the 45 second-hand caravans which were no longer required when the Purbeck camp was converted for student use. He had assumed selling would be a lengthy process and when Stephen Smith, trading as Aubergine Caravans made an offer of £35,000 for all 45 caravans, the offer was accepted with alacrity. It was agreed at the outset that Smith would not be pressed for payment for at least six months, thus giving him time to market the caravans. The company had done business on a similar scale with him previously and he was regarded as sufficiently credit-worthy. But when a reminder was sent at the end of the six months the reply was earth-shattering. The letter was concise.

Aubergine Caravans

Lemsbury Park

Upper Breake

Mr Scrivens,
South Coast Holidays Ltd
Salisbury
Wilts

Dear Mr Scrivens,

I regret to inform you that I am unable to continue my business. It is not me who has got into financial difficulties, but a big London dealer who owes me £60,000 has gone bankrupt. It looks as if he'll only be paying about 15p in the pound. I have asked the bank for more funds to tide me over, but they've refused. Worse, they've called in my loan. They have the deeds of the property to fall back on. The proceeds should just about clear their loan. I reckon I will be left with about £4,000 to meet my outstanding accounts. I owe about £68,000 altogether

including yours. I feel I ought to warn you I owe Mr Wyatt
£12,000 for new caravans I purchased from him and he is
claiming he should be paid before you because I've sold his
vans whereas most of yours remain unsold. I think I paid far
too much for your vans.

Yours faithfully,

J Smith

QUESTIONS TO ANSWER
1. What can be gleaned from the statistics which have been
    provided? To what extent is the venture proving more
    profitable than the original holiday camp – on this evidence?
    (Draw appropriate diagrams to illustrate the situation as
    effectively as possible.)
2. What do you see as the merits and demerits of the pricing
    policy being pursued by South Coast Holidays, with its
    division between commercial rates for food and accommodation
    and 'cost-covering' tuition fees?
3. How would you have reacted to the letter from the insurance
    company? To what extent do you think the company would be
    able to dispute the compensation being offered? What are the
    legal principles involved?
4. What will be the effect of Stephen Smith's bankruptcy? How
    much is South Coast Holidays likely to receive from the
    Receiver in Bankruptcy, according to the figures mentioned
    here? What precautions should they take to make sure their
    interests are protected? Is there any substance in Mr Wyatt's
    contentions? What is the legal position with regard to
    'consideration'? What accounting entries will be required?
    How will the situation be reflected in the final accounts?
5. How do you think the company might profitably use the
    recently vacated Bedford and Exeter Caravan Parks?

WRITTEN ASSIGNMENT
As the executive assistant of Mark Scrivens write a brief report
to him (about 600 words) setting out your recommendations on
how South Coast Holidays might deal with the various problems
confronting them.

13. 'Three's a Crowd . . .'

Scene One
The scene takes place in Peter Paolucci's flat off Carnaby Street in London. He is entertaining two of his friends, both considerably younger than him. Paulette Budge is in her early twenties. After a long spell at art school specialising in dress design, she has recently achieved fame as the winner of a national creative fashion competition. According to the judges of the competition, 'she displays a flair for converting a piece of quite ordinary material into a decidedly exciting and distinctive garment'. She had expected to find herself deluged with orders and propositions but apart from the cheque for the £1000 prize and the initial media publicity, there has been no substantive interest in her success. Her boyfriend, Neil Gunn, is as disappointed as she is about the lack of offers and he has developed his own plans. The three of them are now sitting down over a bottle of Martini, discussing the details.

NEIL: I took Paulette over to see the shop and she likes it. It's tailor-made for us. We'd use the rooms on the first floor as a storeroom and an office. The top floor would be the workroom where we'd have the machines and the seamstresses. We'd be able to provide the machines and organise the women . . . Paulette reckons we'd need six full-timers, but some of the better seamstresses are only available part-time.
PETER: That sounds fine. For my part I'll provide the premises. There's a 21-year lease – with eight years still to run. The rent is £3500 a year excluding rates. I bought the lease for £15,000 last month. I was going to set up a boutique on my own but I like the sound of this. I think we'll do much better if we join forces.
PAULETTE: I want to get started as soon as possible. I've got lots of ideas and if you're going to sell my things exclusively we've got to work up a reasonable stock. I'll put in my prize money to buy the materials I need but I won't be able to pay the wages.
NEIL: Of course not. Peter and I have talked about that. We'll need a bank loan or overdraft to start us off. I'll get that organised tomorrow morning. And I'll have to get to work on advertising and publicity – and of course we'll need some girls to sell the dresses in the shop.
PAULETTE: We'll want more than ordinary salesgirls on this job. Remember we're going to offer the customers free adjustments and alterations. And I'd like to see the girls dressing fashionably. Maybe they could wear my dresses – like models. It would be

worth paying an extra few pounds a week for the right girls.
PETER: And I take it you understand that I shan't be able to
take much part in the day-to-day running of the place. I'll have
to leave it to you two . . . (he turned to Paulette) I expect
Neil has told you I've got two other shops. I'm in antiques
really, but I reckon there's money to be made in dresses too.
And your dresses are no dearer than those the kids buy off the
pegs . . . yet they're different. I think they'll sell like
hot cakes.
PAULETTE: I hope so.
NEIL: Well, let's drink to it anyway. To our new fashion house!
By the way what are we going to call it? Paulette's? Or Penny
Paulette's? Using part of Peter's name and part of mine? It's
something we've got to think about if we're going to open a
bank account. Incidentally you did say you agreed, Peter, that
we should ask them to allow cheques to be drawn on the account
signed by any two of the three of us?

Your first assignment
Assume that Peter Paolucci has taken legal advice. You are then
invited to draft a letter from a firm of solicitors setting out
his rights as a partner and the dangers for him in the present
situation.

Scene Two
This scene takes place just over six months later. The trio are
in the small office on the top floor of their shop. The main
topic of conversation is the young assistant who has been
dismissed.

NEIL: What happened, Peter?
PETER: Well, I knew we were having all sorts of trouble with
our girls, so when you asked me to look after the shop for a
couple of weeks I watched them like a hawk. They didn't like it
I know but they need watching. Anyway, I saw young Julie serving
this weird looking girl. They seemed very friendly and she
bought a couple of the more expensive dresses. I noticed the girl
paid with a Lloyds Bank cheque. She showed a credit card and I
saw Julie make a note of the number on the back of the cheque.
So I thought everything was OK. But later on I went to the
till and the cheque had gone. I challenged her and she showed me
a Midland cheque. She said that was the one the girl had given
her . . . 'What are you suggesting?' she said.
NEIL: What did you say?
PETER: Well, I knew I couldn't prove anything, so I kept quiet
but she knew that I knew. On the Monday she came in late. It
was half past nine and she was half an hour late. I told her
to leave and she left.
PAULETTE: She came back to see me yesterday. She says she was
unfairly dismissed.
PETER: Unfairly dismissed? She's lucky I didn't bring in the
police!

NEIL: She was one of our best salesgirls I thought.
PAULETTE: Yes, she was very popular with the customers.
PETER: No wonder!
NEIL: (diplomatically changing the subject) That reminds me.
Paulette and I have been wondering about how we can get the
girls really motivated. I know a couple of boutiques which offer
their girls bonuses. We could give them 5% or even 10% on sales.
PETER: Won't that cut down our profits - if we make any?
NEIL: Not really. It's just a choice between giving the girls
a flat wage or a mixture of wage and bonus.
PAULETTE: The seamstresses won't be able to get bonuses.
NEIL: Why not?

Scene Three
The final scene takes place one year from the start of the
venture. Neil has produced a trial balance to show to his
partners prior to drawing up the final accounts. Peter is
studying the figures.

	Drawings (£)	Credit (£)
Capital account: P. Budge		1,000
P. Paolucci		15,000
Drawings: P. Budge	2,404	
N. Gunn	3,200	
P. Paolucci	1,000	
Bank loan		10,000
Bank charges	1,356	
Debtors and creditors	98	5,148
Sales less returns		76,375
Purchases less returns	12,717	
Salaries: P. Budge	4,200	
N. Gunn	5,100	
Insurance	243	
Motor vehicle	6,130	
Shop fittings	3,520	
Bank overdraft		512
Leasehold premises	15,000	
Discounts	33	21
Rates	1,969	
Lighting and heating	613	
General expenses	222	
Tools and equipment	400	
Motor expenses	325	
Machines	829	
Wages	48,402	
Advertising	295	
	£108,056	£108,056

Notes: Stock in hand - Materials £1,957
               Made-up dresses £14,956
               Work in progress £934
         £759 of the rates are paid in advance
         The van and fittings are expected to last about ten years

The trio are once again in conversation.

PETER: I'd like to see the accounts when the accountant has
prepared them. There are a few surprises I must admit.
NEIL: I'll let you have a copy as soon as they produce them.
PAULETTE: I'm going to a warehouse at Deptford tomorrow.
There's a consignment of flood-damaged material which is going
really cheap and they're offering six months credit. We could
buy in bulk at a really favourable discount.
PETER: Flood-damaged? Yes, I saw the advertisement in the
newspapers. But you've got to be careful with that sort of deal.
PAULETTE: That's what *we* need to do - advertise. People can't
buy our dresses if they don't know about them.

Your second assignment
Play the role of the partners' accountant. Produce the final
accounts for the first year of trading, on the evidence
available, and write a brief letter to them reporting on the
results.

SOME QUESTIONS TO ANSWER ON THE CASE GENERALLY
1. Can you think of a name which might be suitable for a
    business such as this? A name which might be appealing to
    the young ladies who would be buying the dresses?
2. What sort of advertising do you think the partners might
    indulge in? What sort of constraints would you advise?
3. How do you view the sacking of the salesgirl, Julie? What
    is the legal position?
4. What do you think of the idea of paying the staff bonuses?
    What rate of bonus would you advocate? Do you think group
    bonuses might be preferable?
5. Assuming they both carry the same rate of interest, which
    is the cheaper form of borrowing from the borrowers' point
    of view - the bank loan or the overdraft?
6. How would you deal with the partnership situation if you
    were in Peter Paolucci's shoes?

14. The Takeover

Many people who visit this famous South Coast resort express surprise at the proximity of the two stores so close to each other in the High Street. Sorrell's Store is undoubtedly the town's quality department store. From the inception of the business sixty years ago the Sorrel family proudly provided their wealthy patrons with high-quality merchandise of every sort - from luxury furnishings to the more exclusive blends of tea and coffee. There was even an antiques department which offered Sorrell's clientele the more expensive and rare 'collectors' pieces'.

When J.P. Hardwick and Sons Ltd opened a store a short stone's throw away the Sorrells were unruffled. Hardwicks had a number of stores in the south and catered for what the Sorrells generally described as 'mass tastes'. They provided a wide range of goods too, but for those with less to spend. They aimed at low-priced goods with quick turnovers. Far from taking away each others' business, the stores seemed to function as complements to each other. As Gilbert Sorrell was wont to tell his business associates at the Rotary Club lunches, 'our clients go and look at Hardwick's stuff and are then glad to pay the bit extra we ask for our quality goods!' Perhaps he should have added, in fairness, 'and Hardwick's customers come and look at our store and are then less reluctant to pay the more reasonable prices asked by them for rather similar commodities'.

In any case both stores fluorished initially, though over the years the gulf between the tastes of the wealthy and less wealthy diminished noticeably and gradually drew the two stores into more direct competition with each other. With economic recession and shrinking markets both stores came under pressure and it was no surprise to find a crisis situation developing. It had reached a point where only one of the stores could survive.

For many months it was unclear which of the stores would close down. The first move was made by the Chairman and chief executive of G. Sorrell and Son (Stores) Ltd, John Weekes, the son-in-law of the founder (Gilbert died two years ago and his only son, Dennis, was killed in the war serving in Bomber Command). John made a bid for the adjacent Hardwick site by approaching the owner of the freehold and offering a substantial sum for the same. His hope was that with Hardwick's 21-year lease falling due for renewal in two years' time he might be able to make life difficult for them if he proved to be the freeholder at that time. Unfortunately for him the freeholder responded by informing Hardwick's board of the offer and asking them whether they were interested in topping the offer themselves. Feigning interest the Hardwick board have meanwhile -

through John Weekes - made overtures for a takeover of all the
Sorrell shares.

The plan for amalgamation
The business of the two stores would be amalgamated during the
course of the next two years. At the end of this period the
business would be conducted solely on the existing Sorrell site.
John Weekes would, as from now, receive a salary of £40,000 a year
and a five-year contract. He would also be given a seat on the
Hardwick board. In payment for their stakes the Sorrell
shareholders are offered £2.50 in cash and three ordinary stock
units in Hardwick for each £1 share in Sorrell's. The Sorrell shares
are held exclusively by members of the family together with a
few long-serving company executives as indicated in Table 14.1.

TABLE 14.1

Shareholder	No. of shares
John Weekes	4,000
Maxine Weekes (John's wife)	20,000
Linda Sorrell (Gilbert's widow - his second wife)	25,000
Edward Critchlow (Chief Accountant/Director)	15,000
Robin Petchford (Chief Buyer/Director)	11,000
Edward Critchlow and Lewis Graham (Solicitor) as Trustees of the estate of the late Gilbert Sorrell (held in trust for infant grandchildren)	25,000

YOUR ASSIGNMENT
The latest balance sheets for both companies are given in Tables
14.2 and 14.3, together with other relevant statistics. On the
evidence available you are asked to consider the implications from
the point of view of:

(1) the various shareholders in Sorrells bearing in mind their
    differing interests;
(2) the shareholders of Hardwick's and the effect of the
    amalgamation on their interests;
(3) the board of directors of Hardwick's, particularly the
    problems which might be anticipated under the headings of:
    (a) staff
    (b) future organisation structure
    (c) future business policy.

Additional information is given in Table 14.4 and Figures 14.1
and 14.2.

TABLE 14.2   Balance sheet as at 30 June 198-: G. Sorrell and Son (Stores) Ltd

	(£)		(£)
Ordinary shares of £1 each fully paid	100,000	*Fixed assets*	
General reserves	900,000	Freehold property (1980 valuation)	1,025,000
Dividend equalisation fund	82,370	Fittings and equipment less depreciation	80,696
Balance on profit and loss acount	3,612	Motor vehicles less depreciation	53,635
	1,085,982		1,159,331
Current liabilities		*Current assets*	
Bank loan 383,245		Cash and bank balances	1,862
accrued interest 11,235	394,480	Sundry debtors	92,513
Taxation outstanding	48,984	Stocks at cost	400,365
Sundry creditors	126,378	Prepaid accounts	1,753
	569,842		496,493
	1,655,824		1,655,824

Sales, profits and dividends over past five years

	Year 1	Year 2	Year 3	Year 4	Year 5 (to 30 June last)
Sales (£000s)	1,735	1,923	2,084	1,845	1,901
Net Profit (£000s)	245	195	183	159	168
Dividends (%)	80	80	75	70	60

81

TABLE 14.3   Balance sheet as at 30 September 198-: J.P. Hardwick and Sons Plc (previous year's figures in brackets)

	(£000)	(£000)
Fixed assets	3,216	(3,150)
Goodwill	117	(117)
Current assets	3,015	(3,042)
Total assets	6,348	(6,309)
less current liabilities	2,398	(2,343)
	3,950	(3,966)
Financed by		
Ordinary stock units of 25p each	2,000	(2,000)
8% cumulative preference stock units of £1 each	200	(200)
Reserves	712	(702)
	2,912	(2,902)
11½% mortgage debenture stock	750	(750)
Deferred taxation	288	(314)
	3,950	(3,966)

Notes:
1. Dividends on ordinary stock have been 4% per annum in each of the last four years.
2. The middle price of the ordinary stock units on the Stock Exchange has averaged 20p during the past twelve months.

TABLE 14.4   Staff employed in the two stores

	Sorrells		Hardwicks	
	male	female	male	female
Manager grade	29	4	11	12
Sales staff (full-time)	61	39	23	98
(part-time)	0	0	0	34
Office staff	3	11	3	6
Storemen and drivers	6	0	3	0
Lift operators	0	8	0	0

Notes:

1. Sorrells have managers (and assistant managers) responsible for staff and day-to-day management on each floor. Managers are also appointed for each department and assume responsibility for buying the goods sold in their respective departments. Buying is undertaken in the Hardwick organisation by a small team of buyers based on the head office in London. Hardwick's

have fewer departments and although the departmental managers are described as buyers their function is essentially to order goods from catalogues/price lists provided by their head office.

2. Sorrell's sales staff are paid approximately 10% more than Hardwick's sales staff of similar age and experience, but other staff (including managers) are paid broadly comparable salaries/wages. Sorrell's staff also have the benefit of a non-contributory pension scheme which gives them a pension at the age of 60 equal to 1% of their salary/wages for every year they are employed by the company.

3. Sixteen of Sorrell's managers (including all four females) are over the age of 55.

4. Sorrell's window dressing is done by an outside agency while the Hardwick store has a team which comes from the head office to perform this operation.

5. One explanation for the extra clerical staff employed by Sorrell's is that the store operates an interest-free credit service whereby any goods exceeding £200 in value can be paid for over a period of six months or twelve months. By contrast, hire purchase agreements for Hardwick's goods are arranged through a local finance company.

FIGURE 14.1   Floor Plans for Hardwick's Store

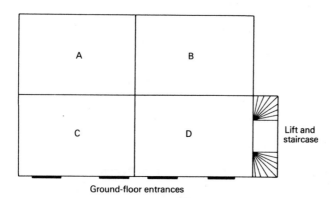

Ground-floor entrances

Basement: A/B   Stores/delivery bay
              C/D   Teenager boutique/coffee bar
Ground floor: 'Under £10' - all goods on this floor below this
                  price (aimed at impulse purchasing)
First floor: A/C   Ladies' wear
                 B   Children's wear
                 D   Men's wear
Second floor: A/C   Audio/visual entertainment
                  B/D   Toys/games/sports goods
Third floor: A/B   Furniture/soft furnishings
                 C/D   Electrical goods
Fourth floor: A/B/D   Restaurant
                  C   Offices

83

FIGURE 14.2   Floor Plans for Sorrell's Store

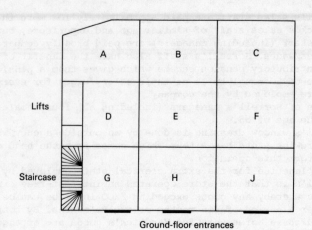

A	B	C
Lifts	D	E	F
Staircase	G	H	J

Ground-floor entrances

Basement:	A/B	Gardening
	C	Garden furniture
	D/E	Sports goods
	F/J	Radio/television
	G/H	Records
Ground floor:	A/B/C	Soft furnishings
	D	Hosiery
	E	Cosmetics
	F/J	Gifts/jewellery
	G/H	Tobacco/confections
First floor:	A	Baby wear
	B/C	Men's wear

Remainder of floor - ladies' wear

Second floor:	A	Photographic equipment
	D/G	Bookshop
	E	Chinaware
	F	Glassware
	H/J	Travel agency
Third floor:	A/B/C	Furniture
	D/G	Kitchen equipment
	E/F/H/J	Carpets
Fourth floor:	A/B	Offices
	C/F	Accounts
	D/E/G/H	Antiques
	J	Paintings

15.   The Hong Kong Options

The 99-year lease under which Britain gained possession of the
Crown Colony of Hong Kong from the old Chinese Imperial
Government expires on 30 June 1997. Although the total land area
is only just over 400 square miles its entrepot role is enhanced
when it is recognised as the gateway to China, a virtually
untapped market of more than 800 million people.

On the other side of the Eurasian landmass the directors of
G. Robinson (Agricultural Engineers) Ltd have Hong Kong very
much on their minds at the present time. The story starts two
years ago when 'Craggies' (as they are called in the KTP
Engineering Group - they are a sub-subsidiary) developed a new
power unit for their cultivators. The unit is petrol driven with
a 3 h.p. easy-start engine which is undistinguished in itself,
but it has been designed with a special rotary device which has
been linked to tungsten-treated blades giving the machine a
cutting depth of 18 inches instead of the usual 12 inches for a
hand-held rotovator. The Craggies team accepted they were aiming
for a limited market but introduced a special feature - an
optional 'prehensile switch roller' - which allowed the machine
to be used on steeply sloping ground. They hoped this would open
up some export markets; perhaps Third World countries would find
the new Craggie *Mountaineer* useful on ground inaccessible to
tractors.

The *Mountaineer* was displayed at a number of overseas trade
exhibitions but demonstrations were always difficult and
sometimes impossible. Sales were negligible and Craggies were
beginning to think their new model was still-born. Then they
received a surprise visitor. Mr Frank Soo, the chief executive
of Samuel Chan and Son Ltd, import and export merchants based
in Hong Kong, had been asked to put a proposition to Craggies.
'A most important client' had expressed an interest in the
Mountaineer - provided a satisfactory price could be negotiated
for the large numbers contemplated. Group headquarters became
involved and saw all sorts of possibilities. Jack Martin, the
group's representative on the Craggies board, flew out for
prolonged discussions with the Chan directors. KTP were sure
that Chan's 'important customer' was the Chinese government.
They were asking for 2600 *Mountaineers* per annum over a period of
five years: an order worth over £50 million. KTP saw the
possibility of other sales from the group, while the Chan
company saw the chance to provide KTP with all sorts of plastic
components. The arrangement could be mutually beneficial and a
formal tie-in between the companies was proposed. KTP accepted

that Craggies were primarily associated through the *Mountaineer*
deal and the group board of directors left it to the Craggies
board to choose between the three options which had been given
to them by the Chan company.

Option One – an exchange of shares. A 10% stake in the equity of
Samuel Chan and Son Ltd – the quotation on the Hong Kong Stock
Exchange being HK$ 14.50 per share – in direct exchange for
120,000 new Craggie ordinary stock units, issued to Samuel Chan
or his nominee. As part of this deal it was agreed that the London
representative of the Chan company, a Mr John Lee, would be given
a place on the board of Craggies, while KTP would nominate one
of their Far Eastern representatives for the board of Samuel Chan
and Son Ltd.
    The Chan shares would be provided by Samuel Chan who either
owns directly – or through his family – 40% of the voting shares.
There are no other known shareholders with more than 5% of the
voting shares. A condition imposed by the group directors is that
if this option were adopted the rate of dividend on the enlarged
capital would have to be sustained.
Option Two – an issue of debentures. The proposal is that
Craggies would issue £100,000 10½% mortgage debenture stock to be
taken up entirely by Samuel Chan and Son. In effect it would be a
long-term loan from the Hong Kong company aimed at providing some
of the additional funds needed to expand production to the
required level. The Trust Deed would appoint the Hong Kong and
Shanghai Banking Corporation as trustees and give them the right
to sell the company's factory in East Anglia if the interest
payments were ever more than three months in arrears. This would
be coupled with a floating charge on the company's other assets
and meanwhile the deeds of title to the land on which the factory
stands would be deposited with the trustees' London office. The
debentures would be redeemable at the end of the five years – and
transferable, either wholly or in part (£1 units).

Option Three – no financial tie-in with the Hong Kong merchants.
This proposal would be simply based on the contract to be
entered into with the Chan company for the supply of
Mountaineers. The price is fixed at HK$ 4200 per machine Free on
Board, subject to monthly delivery dates of even quantities
throughout the five-year period.

YOUR FIRST ASSIGNMENT
Choose between the options justifying your conclusions. Further
information follows.

The KTP group of companies
The group are principally involved in engineering. Some of their
subsidiaries are shown in Table 15.1.

TABLE 15.1

Name of company	Location	Major activities	Annual turnover (£s mill.)
Apex Construction	South Wales	Roadworks, bridges and quarrying	18.5
Borodin Marine	South Wales	Marine repairs	2.8
R. Brown & Sons (Engineering)	South Wales	Manufacture of cranes and excavators	7.1
Chapman & Bridges	London	Building and construction	30.0
F. Fleishman (Transport)	Home Counties	Heavy transport	1.9
KTP (Australia)	Sydney	General construction	11.5
KTP (Nigeria)	Lagos	Building construction and distribution	7.6
C. Robinson (Agricultural Engineers)	East Anglia	Agricultural machinery	8.5
Round & Tebbit	East Anglia	Reconditioned tractors	3.7
Standish & Co.	South Wales	Mining and marine water pumps	11.5
Underwood Engineering	South Wales	Machine tools	5.8

C. Robinson (Agricultural Engineers)
The Craggies management team have produced a variety of
information aimed at helping the board of directors to reach
a decision.

TABLE 15.2   A four-weekly cost schedule for cultivators at present
prices (in £000)

Level of production	Materials and components			Wages			Fuel, etc.		
	MR	WH	WM	MR	WH	WM	MR	WH	WM
200	10.0	9.0	8.0	16.0	14.5	14.0	2.1	1.9	1.8
250	12.5	9.9	8.8	17.3	16.0	15.4	2.2	2.0	1.9
300	15.0	10.9	9.7	18.5	17.5	16.8	2.3	2.1	2.0
350	17.5	12.0	10.7	19.6	19.0	18.2	2.4	2.2	2.1
400	20.0	13.2	11.8	20.6	20.5	19.7	2.5	2.3	2.2
450	22.5	14.5	13.0	21.7	22.0	21.2	2.6	2.4	2.3
500	25.0	16.0	14.3	22.9	23.5	22.7	2.7	2.5	2.4
550	27.5	17.6	15.7	24.3	25.0	24.3	2.9	2.6	2.4
600	30.0	19.4	17.3	26.0	26.5	26.0	3.0	2.7	2.5
650	32.5	21.3	19.0	28.0	28.0	27.8	3.1	2.8	2.6
700	35.0	23.4	20.9	30.3	29.5	29.7	3.2	2.9	2.7

Fixed costs are estimated at £100,000 whatever the level of production. 700 machines are the maximum output for any of the models on any of the production lines. The *Workhorse* (WH) is the standard model. It was made exclusively on production line no. 1 last year. The *Workmaid* (WM) is designed for use in smaller gardens and working areas. Switching production from one model to another on any particular line is technically possible. The estimated cost of a switch is £30,000 at present prices.

FIGURE 15.1   Factory layout

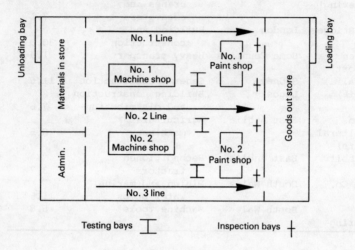

FIGURE 15.2   Marketing mix

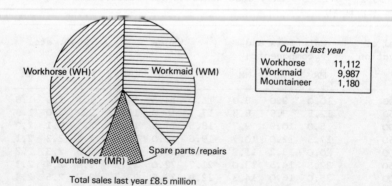

Output last year	
Workhorse	11,112
Workmaid	9,987
Mountaineer	1,180

Total sales last year £8.5 million

TABLE 15.3 Abbreviated balance sheet as at 31 March 198-:
C. Robinson (Agricultural Engineers) Ltd

	(£s mill.)		(£s mill.)
Ordinary stock units		*Fixed assets*	
of £1 each	2.0	Premises (at cost 1968)	1.5
Reserves (including		Vehicles and machinery	
balance on profit		(less depreciation)	1.2
and loss account)	1.6		
Stockholders' stake	3.6		2.7
Current liabilities		*Current assets*	
Loan from group (at		Debtors	1.7
10% p.a.) 0.5		Stocks	0.4
Creditors 0.2		Cash	0.1
			2.2
Bank loan			
(including			
accrued			
interest) 0.6	1.3		
	4.9		4.9

Notes:

1. Average over past five years – net sales £8.5 million; net
   profit £.6 million.
2. The ordinary dividend has been 20% gross for each of the last
   five years.

TABLE 15.4 Abbreviated balance sheet as at 31 January 198-:
Samuel Chan and Son Ltd

	(HK$ mill.)		(HK$ mill.)
Ordinary shares of		*Fixed assets*	
HK$10 each	12.5		
Reserves including		Leasehold warehouse	
balance on profit		(7-year lease –	
and loss account	3.1	5 years to run)	7.7
Shareholders' stake	15.6	Vehicles	1.1
Leasehold redemption		Motor vessels	10.8
reserve	2.2	Other vessels	3.1
12% debentures	5.0		
			22.7
Current liabilities			
Creditors 15.7			
Loan from Mr S.		*Current assets*	
Chan (at 6%			
p.a) 0.5		Debtors 10.7	
Bank overdraft 0.6	16.8	Stocks 6.2	16.9
	39.6		39.6

Notes:

1. Average over past five years – net sales HK$ 165 million
   – net profit HK$ 38 million
   – ordinary dividends 28%

YOUR SECOND ASSIGNMENT
Consider the threats and opportunities in this situation from Craggies' point of view. What use could be made of the Export Credits Guarantee Department of the Department of Trade? What other ideas can you offer for eliminating or minimising the risks?

16. Z12 Insect Repellent

Frank Robson is a research chemist with one of the major oil
companies. He has been the project leader involved in commercially
exploiting certain by-products which have emerged from a
research programme aimed at converting coal and lignite into a
form of petroleum suitable for use in the internal combustion
engine. A technique for conversion has been found and a plant has
been set up in Zambia to produce limited supplies of the new
fuel from locally mined coal. The main deterrent to a large-scale
conversion programme is that the cost of the new fuel is
estimated to be approximately 15% higher than the price of oil in
the open market at the present time. Nevertheless, the company
feel that it is expedient to set up the Zambian plant and at the
same time continue their experiments in the hope that the costs
of conversion might yet be reduced.

One of the by-products which has come out of the conversion
process is a substance which has been found to be repellent to
all forms of insect (as well as many of the smaller rodents).
The researchers have code-named this product Z12 and Frank
Robson has been given the responsibility for exploiting it
commercially. At this point of time a wholly owned subsidiary
of the oil company has been incorporated - Repela Ltd. A factory
has been acquired on an industrial estate on the outskirts of
Southampton and it is planned to produce Z12 in aerosol cans
(75 ml, 215 ml and 550 ml sizes). The large size is being
considered for use in factories and offices, etc.

Z12 is being combined with an emulsifying agent and a
rubberised latex which are comparatively inexpensive. The product
is transparent and odourless. The proposed constituents are:
emulsifier 82.5%, rubberised latex 10.5%, Z12 7.0%. The research
established that by spraying an area such as a door or window
surround with the compound, insects of all sorts will not only
avoid contact with the treated area but will not approach within
approximately one metre. Laboratory tests were carried out in a
total of 1000 separate trials. In each case a 20 ml application
was applied to a variety of surfaces (wood, metal and plastic)
around 3 m x 2 m apertures. The product was tested in a variety
of situations and was generally able to withstand adverse weather
conditions though temperatures affected the results as shown in
Figure 16.1.

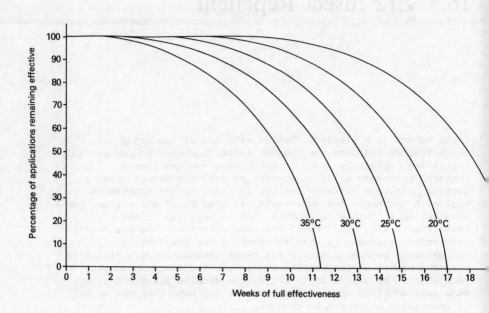

Finance

The oil company accepts that they do not have contacts with
the appropriate retail outlets and so they are joining forces
with an equally large multinational chemical group with a
widespread distribution network. The chemical group are prepared
to invest £250,000 in the project to add to the £500,000 the
oil company consider they have already staked. Three alternative
capital structures are being contemplated.

Option One: 500,000 ordinary shares of £1 each (owned by oil
company). £250,000 10% mortgage debenture stock (to be purchased
by the chemical group at par and against the security of the
London factory).
Option Two: 700,000 ordinary shares of £1 each (500,000 owned
by oil company, the remainder being purchased by the chemical
group at £1.25 per share).
Option Three: 500,000 ordinary shares of £1 each (300,000 owned
by the oil company, the remainder being purchased by the
chemical group at £1.25 per share). £200,000 10% debentures
(owned by the oil company).

The oil company have not yet approached the chemical group but are considering the possibilities before negotiations take place.

Cost structure
The oil company is to supply Z12 to Repela Ltd at a price of £1 per litre, rising by 10% per annum over the next five years. Supplies are limited, however, to 15,000 litres per annum. The chemical group will also be major suppliers. They have agreed to supply Repela necessary items at what they describe as 'most-favoured customer' prices, at present:

> Emulsifier: 70p per litre
> Latex: £1.20 per litre
> Aerosol cans*: 75ml : 15p
> 215ml : 20p
> 550ml : 25p

*These will be provided by one of the subsidiaries within the chemical group.

The fixed costs are calculated at £250,000 per annum, to include depreciation charges and advertising expenditure. The remaining (variable) costs have been calculated on a unit basis. The schedule discloses that a 215 ml can costs 20% more than a 75 ml can, while a 550 ml can costs 25% more than a 215 ml can - in terms of these additional costs. The schedule is as follows:

> 75 ml can = 1 unit
> 215 ml can = 1.2 units
> 550 ml can = 1.5 units

On this basis Figure 16.2 can be used to determine the variable costs at different levels of production.

FIGURE 16.2   Variable costs (wages/miscellaneous) at different
levels of production

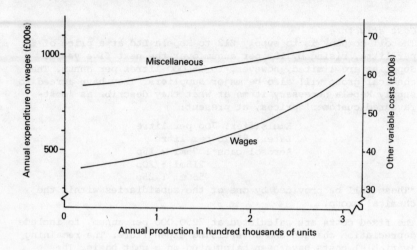

Marketing
The competing products at the present time are solid-form
repellents which are for use in enclosed spaces. They have the
effect of killing flying insects which come within 'striking
distance'. The chemical company which is helping to finance
Repela Ltd is market leader in insect repellents and currently
has a 45% share of the UK market and an estimated 4% of the
world market. A market research agency, associated with the
chemical company, has been consulted and their report includes
estimates of the annual sales (see Table 16.1) which could be
expected at a given range of prices to compete with existing
products, assuming an annual expenditure of £100,000 on
advertising as presently budgeted.
The report advises:

We feel that the different sized aerosol cans on offer would
be aimed at quite separate segments of the market, the house-
wife purchasing in the supermarket would go for the small
cans, while the large cans could only be expected to appeal to
industrial users. Thus, one could not expect to find increased
sales of small cans because the larger cans were discontinued.
    The technological superiority of the product would seem to
lie in the fact that it is possible to spray all window- and
door-frames in an average sized house with the contents of a
75 ml can and thereby be bluebottle, wasp free and even ant
free for virtually the whole of summer. One also assumes
environmentalists will be pleased to hear that Z12 does not
kill insects. It does not seem to be harmful to humans or
pets in any way which is an advantage over some competing
products.
    There is always an initial problem of drawing the attention
of the public to a new product and the proposed advertising
budget in this case precludes a sustained television

TABLE 16.1   Sales forecast for Repela Ltd insect repellent

	Price to be charged to wholesalers	Suggested mark-up	Price to be charged to retailers	Suggested mark-up	Price to be charged to public	Annual sales of cans in thousands
75 ml cans	70p	21p	91p	27p	£1.18	800
	80p	24p	£1.04	31p	£1.35	700
	90p	27p	£1.17	35p	£1.52	550
	£1.00	30p	£1.30	39p	£1.69	300
215 ml cans	£2.00	60p	£2.60	78p	£3.38	240
	£2.20	66p	£2.86	86p	£3.72	200
	£2.40	72p	£3.12	94p	£4.06	150
	£2.60	78p	£3.38	£1.01	£4.39	100
550 ml cans	£3.50	£1.40	£4.90	£1.96	£6.86	180
	£4.00	£1.60	£5.60	£2.24	£7.84	170
	£4.50	£1.80	£6.30	£2.52	£8.82	160
	£5.00	£2.00	£7.00	£2.80	£9.80	150

advertising campaign. This leaves us with a number of ploys to introduce the repellent to the market, namely:

(1) Selected supermarkets and food shops to be given demonstrations of the effectiveness of the product with maximum attendant publicity.
(2) The product to be offered at a special price in a women's magazine. The magazine we have in mind has a weekly circulation of 300,000 per week and offers us especially favourable rates - £5000 for a full-page spread so long as the editor is assured that the price we are asking is at least 25% below the normal retail price.
(3) A simple competition could be organised with, say, £10,000 prize money - forms available at the retail outlets. As a variation from the usual format for competitions the prizes might go to the retailers themselves, say, one entry form per gross pack. There are problems in this but they do not seem insurmountable and it is certainly the retailers on whom we depend to push sales.

No doubt you will have some more ideas on the subject.

From our experience with similar products it seems likely that the sales of this new line will be concentrated in the summer months for the United Kingdom sales. Figure 16.3 shows the pattern of sales which might be predicted.

FIGURE 16.3

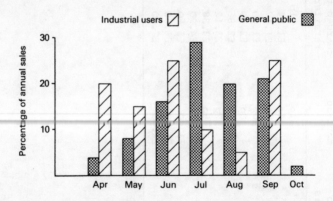

QUESTIONS TO BE ANSWERED
1. What sort of production would you advocate for Repela Ltd on this evidence? How would you divide your production effort between 75 ml, 215 ml and 550 ml cans? To what extent would you describe the demand for the new product as elastic?
2. At what level of production would revenue begin to exceed costs? (Draw a break-even chart to illustrate the point and explain its significance.)
3. Which of the options set out on page 92 would be preferable from the oil company's point of view? What are the various implications? How do you think the problem of capitalisation might be resolved equitably?

4. Which features of the new product would you emphasise in the advertising campaign? Under what name would you suggest the new product be marketed? Which groups do you think would be most likely to buy the product? How, when and where do you think the product would best be advertised? Be as specific as possible.
5. A product like this is bound to attract complaints of one sort or another from the various users. What sorts of complaints would you expect to predominate? Are there any serious risks? To what extent do you think such risks might be either reduced or entirely eliminated?
6. What do you see as the major problems facing Frank Robson as chief executive? What are the short-term problems? And the longer-term problems?

17. Diana Cosmetics Plc

This company is situated in the London area. There are three operating units within a circumference of three miles. The so-called Denby Cross plant is the production unit and concentrates on a comparatively narrow range of cosmetics. The Shenton plant, half a mile away, manufactures the various plastic tubes and containers required by Denby Cross, while the warehouse at Crimford is the materials store and the distribution depot for the finished products. The striking containers are a feature of Diana Cosmetics and the products are designed to appeal to the teenage and 'less sophisticated' markets.

Among the senior executives there are two women which is no doubt befitting an organisation which is catering for an exclusively female clientele. The Marketing Manager is Meera Jehan whose family came over from Kenya in the 1970s. It was she who spotted the possibility of retailing Diana Cosmetics through boutiques. It was a simple idea - but a winner. After all, the young ladies who visited the boutiques were the very people for whom the Diana range of cosmetics was created. Last year the sales reached a record £2.8 million. 60% of all products sold on the home market are now sold through boutiques. The nature of the marketing mix can be gleaned from Figure 17.1.

FIGURE 17.1   Analysis of sales by product for last year

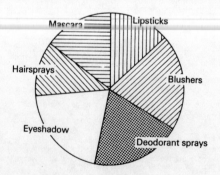

The other female playing a central role in the organisation is Susan Thorpe who is the Personnel Manager. A female in this post has obvious advantages since 80% of the workforce is female and drawn from the younger elements of the population. The extent of Susan's responsibilities is evidenced by the statistics shown in Table 17.1.

TABLE 17.1   Analysis of workforce (including administrative staff)

Sex/Age		Denby Cross	Shenton	Crimford
Female:	under 21 yrs	188	9	3
	21–30 yrs	133	5	0
	31–40 yrs	88	0	0
	41–50 yrs	32	3	0
	over 50 yrs	1	1	0
Male:	under 21 yrs	5	18	11
	21–30 yrs	17	15	15
	31–40 yrs	11	5	3
	41–50 yrs	3	5	2
	over 50 yrs	1	2	2
Totals		479	63	36

The scene
Meera and Susan are visiting Bill Maycock, the Production Manager designate, in his office. He joined the firm last week and is due to take over his duties as chief executive when the incumbent retires next month. The meeting has been suggested so that they can exchange ideas and discuss problems of common interest. Over a cup of coffee the trio complete the social introductions and then get down to business.

BILL: (to Susan) So you have been here from the start?
SUSAN: Yes. When I came in October 1978 there was only the Denby Cross plant in operation. And I had the job of recruiting the first girls for the production lines.
BILL: Did you deliberately go for the younger girls? I notice the girls on the shop floor are still rather young.
SUSAN: It wasn't a conscious decision but it was mainly school-leavers who applied for the jobs when we advertised and so we ended up with a rather young workforce.
BILL: Since the average age is still very low I suppose that means most of them don't stay.
SUSAN: Well, you've got to accept that the jobs they do are pretty boring - filling up lipstick moulds, fixing tiny mascara brushes to applicators. But we don't lose that many of them. The labour turnover is about 25% in the company as a whole - it's higher among the girls obviously, especially the younger ones.
BILL: Yes, I can see that. I must admit it was one of my first reactions when I saw the production lines. You'd expect more automation: there's an awful lot of old-fashioned machinery still operating.
MEERA: I can give you one explanation for that. It's often cropped up at our monthly brainstorming sessions - all the senior executives get together once a month for a deliberately wide-ranging discussion. We have to cater for a constantly changing market. Our current best-seller is the new Multi-colour Hair Spray - you might have seen them at work on number three production line. We can't get enough of them at the moment. It's a craze. Lots of girls use more than one colour; we've even got

99

a rainbow streak. But next week the craze will be over and it will be something completely different they want. This comparatively labour-intensive style of production is suited to the batch production we need here.

BILL: I can see that. But it means we have to put up with the problems of boredom on the production line. (Turning again to Susan) What sort of absenteeism do we get?

SUSAN: I've got one set of figures with me. Yes, here we are. For the company as a whole last month - twenty working days - we lost a total of 1905 days. The under 21s accounted for 1500 of those lost days - there's no difference between males and females though.

BILL: What sorts of things have you tried?

SUSAN: We've tried a bit of job rotation from time to time but it doesn't seem to do any good. And we tried giving them piped music. They said it got on their nerves after a few weeks of it. To be truthful innovations like that haven't been encouraged very much.

BILL: Well I'd certainly like to know what ideas you've got to reduce absenteeism. I don't think we should ever give up trying to make improvements.

SUSAN: I'm delighted to hear you say that. I've got plenty of ideas I'd like to try. I think we could employ some part-timers. We haven't got any part-timers on the payroll. I'd like to introduce good-timekeeping bonuses . . . and a works council.

BILL: A works council? That's not a bad idea - I don't know how you'd organise it mind you. Of course, you don't have unions to contend with do you?

SUSAN: No, but a number of the drivers and storemen at Crimford are members of the Transport and General Workers Union.

MEERA: I think the lunch hours are too long. I've heard quite a few of the girls saying they would prefer shorter lunch hours and earlier finishes.

SUSAN: The problem is the canteen. They need an hour to cope - nearly everyone stays for lunch.

MEERA: I'm not surprised. The firm subsidises the meals to such a large extent - 50% of the cost isn't it?

BILL: What are the hours again?

SUSAN: The morning session starts at 8.30 and goes through to 12.30. After lunch they work from 1.30 to 5.30 with quarter-hour breaks at 10.30 and 3.30. The office staff start later of course. They start at 9.00 and have lunch from 12.00 to 12.30. I'd like to see a late shift introduced so that we could recruit some older women - say 6 till 10.00 at night. And perhaps we will be able to introduce a creche at some time in the future - a playgroup on the premises, for young mothers with children. I'm sure that's a possibility here.

BILL: Great! You've got a useful battery of ideas there. I'm all for getting the rate of absenteeism down. I notice we don't pay anyone when they're absent - except office staff - until they've been with the firm three years. Look, Susan, let me have your ideas in writing. Draft me a brief report. Just an outline plan, that's all I'm asking for. Something that I can consider over the next few weeks. If any of the ideas seem worth trying I'm quite prepared to put them forward to the board of directors.

But I'd like you to concentrate on the advantages that we could expect if they were implemented. Remember I've got to persuade the directors that the ideas are worth further investigation. Of course I'd also like to know the problems that are likely to be encountered.

MEERA: I've got some ideas too!

BILL: (turning to her) I hope you have!

MEERA: I'm frustrated because we sell such a small percentage of our sales overseas - just 10% last year - nearly all of that to Belgium and the Netherlands.

BILL: What's the problem do you think?

MEERA: We don't have the facilities for market research.

BILL: It is a rather small organisation.

MEERA: I appreciate that but I'd like to do my own research. I'd like to make a few trips . . . to have a look at some of the potential markets.

BILL: (chuckling) A world tour at the firm's expense? Seriously though, that seems reasonable enough. But you would have to justify a trip like that. You'd have to let me know precisely what you intended to do. You'd have to put a ceiling on the cost of the trip and explain what you think the company would get out of it. And I think you should concentrate on a particular city or country in the first place. If the first trip proves worthwhile, then we can look for other trips.

MEERA: Talking about money leads me to my other major problem. This is one that my sales reps are always complaining about. We are running up against a number of bad debts. We sell a lot of Diana products to these small boutiques. And yes, we do well out of it. Then every now and again we come up against a dud. They either take ages to pay their bills or they don't pay at all - and my saleswomen are expected to sort it all out.

BILL: What sort of checks do the reps make when they accept an order?

MEERA: It's left to their discretion. Anything up to £100 they can put through without any questions being asked. Otherwise the order has to be referred to me. But we're under pressure to sell and I think the accounting department should set up some sort of credit control system.

BILL: Don't we have anything like that at present?

MEERA: No, and you see the problem is made worse because we don't offer any cash discount if the customer does pay promptly. There's no incentive.

BILL: What sort of discount would you propose?

MEERA: I haven't worked it out precisely . . .

BILL: Well look ladies, I'd be only too glad to put some of these ideas to the board. I ask you both to put your ideas in writing. Do remember that I've only just arrived and that Rome wasn't built in a day.

YOUR ASSIGNMENT
Write reports such as might have been submitted to the new chief executive by his personnel manager and marketing manager.
Optional treatment   If you are working in a group situation, exchange reports and examine one another's work critically. Point out the merits and demerits constructively.

18.   Strike Now — Pay Later

C. Buchan (Marine) Ltd is a comparatively small subsidiary in an
international engineering group. The long-established works are
on Clydeside and used to produce marine pumps for the shipbuilding
industry. However the decline of shipbuilding on the Clyde has
forced them to seek out new products and markets, and since 1975
they have manufactured and marketed a range of outboard motors,
essentially for inshore fishing and leisure craft. In a highly
competitive market they have nevertheless managed to carve a
niche for themselves. They have done so largely on the strength
of the design of their machines which are particularly fuel-
efficient and reliable in all sorts of weather conditions. For
the first few years after the introduction of the *Sea-Bee*
outboard motors the main problem was one of producing enough
units to meet the demand, but those halcyon days are certainly
over and during the past three years competitors in the United
States and Japan have produced models matching Buchans in both
quality and price. Buchans reckoned that they had captured 55%
of the domestic market at one stage but this share has been
substantially eroded since the introduction of the competing
models.

Six months ago William (Billy) MacDougall was appointed
General Manager of Buchans. He joined the company as an apprentice
straight from school twenty-five years ago and has served in
virtually every capacity in the works since that time. He is
very popular with the men (apart from a handful of office staff
the workforce is exclusively male) and has made a point since
becoming assistant general manager of going on to the shop floor
from time to time to 'pass the time of day' with the various
workers. One of the most unpleasant tasks he has had to perform
since his promotion has been to shed 100 of the workforce (the
redundancies were the result of a combination of falling sales and
the introduction of more sophisticated machinery). But his brief
from the holding company has been unambiguous. His objectives
are:

(1) to achieve an increase of at least 10% in sales over the
    next two years;
(2) to provide a return on capital employed of at least 10% per
    annum;
(3) to repay the loan given by the holding company in 1978 to
    assist in an expansion programme at that time.

It has been made clear to MacDougall that his retention as
general manager will depend on his performance in relation to

these targets. He is understandably concerned then when the sales statistics shown in Table 18.1 are provided for him.

TABLE 18.1   Quarterly sales over past two years (£000s)

Machine	Quarter	Up to Dec. 31 last	Previous year
Sea-Bee Cadet (5 hp)	1	398.7	365.4
	2	588.9	534.8
	3	602.5	588.5
	4	387.4	380.0
Sea-Bee Queen (10 hp)	1	504.6	503.8
	2	597.5	589.2
	3	599.1	576.3
	4	388.9	409.1
Sea-Bee Major (15 hp)	1	183.9	203.7
	2	199.5	202.1
	3	196.9	203.8
	4	95.6	185.7
Sea-Bee Giant (25 hp)	1	65.2	63.8
	2	75.9	70.6
	3	80.3	81.0
	4	48.7	35.8

The sales manager has expressed his opinion that the poor results are largely the result of the price increases for all models made necessary by the 12% pay awards negotiated by the men's unions last year. As he puts it, 'We've got an elastic demand curve for our products since the Japanese and the Americans introduced their new models. Even a small increase in price pushes down our sales disproportionately especially since their prices are not going up like ours. My boys are having to sell a virtually identical product at a 10% higher price. It's an uphill struggle!'

The chief accountant has provided a copy of the accounts as anticipated for 31 December next. The figures have been extracted from the master budget and are shown in Tables 18.2 to 18.5. The final accounts for 31 December last are shown in brackets.

TABLE 18.2   Manufacturing account for year to 31 December (£000s)

	For Dec. 31 next	For Dec. 31 last		For Dec. 31 next	For Dec. 31 last
	(£)	(£)		(£)	(£)
Stock of raw materials 1 Jan.	333	(120)	Production cost of goods completed c/d	2,928	(2,414)
Add purchases	1,095	(1,156)			
Carriage inwards	38	(37)			
	1,466	(1,313)			
Less stock of raw materials, 31 Dec.	257	(333)			
Cost of raw materials consumed	1,209	(980)			
Direct labour	827	(551)			
Direct expenses	29	(27)			
Prime cost	2,065	(1,558)			
Factory overheads	407	(423)			
Indirect labour	460	(435)			
	2,932	(2,416)			
Add work in progress 1 Jan	38	(36)			
	2,970	(2,452)			
Less work in progress 31 Dec	42	(38)			
	2,928	(2,414)		2,928	(2,414)

TABLE 18.3　　Profit and loss account

	(£)	(£)		(£)	(£)
Stock of finished goods, 1 Jan.	747	(726)	Sales	4,990	(5,014)
Add production cost of goods completed b/d	2,928	(2,414)			
	3,675	(3,140)			
Less stock of finished goods 31 Dec.	1,052	(747)			
	2,623	(2,393)			
Gross profit c/d	2,367	(2,621)			
	4,990	(5,014)		4,990	(5,014)
Salaries:			Gross profit b/d	2,367	(2,621)
administrative	812	(701)			
sales staff	531	(488)			
Administrative expenses	212	(201)			
Distribution expenses	103	(96)			
Other expenses	73	(65)			
Net profit c/d	636	(1,070)			
	2,367	(2,621)		2,367	(2,621)

TABLE 18.4　　Appropriation account

	(£)	(£)		(£)	(£)
Dividends	400	(600)	Net profit b/d	636	(1,070)
Transfer to reserve	337	(508)	Balance c/d	101	(38)
	737	(1,108)		737	(1,108)

TABLE 18.5   Balance sheet (£000s)

	As at Dec. 31 next	As at Dec. 31 last		As at Dec. 31 next	As at Dec. 31 last
	(£)	(£)		(£)	(£)
Ordinary stock			Fixed assets	1,998	(2,178)
units of £1 each	2,000	(2,000)	Current		
General reserves	1,050	(542)	assets	2,429	(2,231)
	3,050	(2,542)			
Loan from holding					
company	300	(300)			
Current liabilities	979	(1,466)			
Profit and loss	98	(101)			
	4,427	(4,409)		4,427	(4,409)

One of the problems confronting Billy MacDougall is a claim
for increased wages submitted by the principal union representing
the workforce. They are claiming an increase of 20% for all their
members. Negotiations are in progress at national level and
although there is little he can do to influence the situation he
knows how important the outcome is for Buchans - and for his own
career. Since he became general manager he has met the shop
stewards' committee once a month. The meetings are designed to
give the workers' representatives an opportunity to air their
grievances and the chief executive a chance to put forward
management's point of view. At their last meeting he produced the
graph shown in Figure 18.1 and tried to explain what the consequences would be if the workers were to be awarded a substantial
increase in pay. He failed to make any impression on them.

FIGURE 18.1

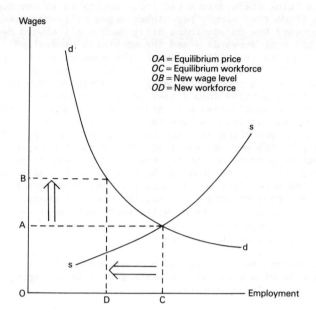

OA = Equilibrium price
OC = Equilibrium workforce
OB = New wage level
OD = New workforce

'The trade unions only achieve wage increases at the expense
of a reduction in the number of workers employed', he told the
group of shop stewards gathered in his office. 'It may be
that those who stay employed benefit, but what about those who
are made redundant . . . and those who would have been given jobs
if the wages hadn't gone up so high?'

The convenor (chief shop steward) was as craggy as he was
cynical. 'What do you want me to do, Mr MacDougall? Do I go out
to my laddies and tell them they can't have any more money but
they can have some graph paper? They won't be able to pay the
rent with that.' He turned to his mates for support and their
wagging heads confirmed his disapproval.

The chief executive was disappointed. He had worked hard to
develop a rapport with the shop stewards but there was no sign
of an *esprit de corps* now that it was needed.

'That's the sort of attitude which is driving us to use more
capital-intensive methods of production. You'll complain like
hell when we introduce robots but you're forcing us into it.
Either that or we'll have to start closing down unprofitable
sections - and that means redundancies for *your* members.'
He wanted them to understand.

One of the younger stewards thumped his fist down on the chief
executive's desk. His eyes were blazing. 'We're entitled to fair
wages', he exploded, 'It's you who force us into strikes. We
don't want to strike but you force us into it!'

YOUR ASSIGNMENT
1. Do you think trade unions can force employers to pay more
   wages or do they simply pay higher wages to fewer workers in
   employment? How do you think Billy MacDougall should deal
   with his shop stewards – and the workforce generally?
2. What would be the effect of wage increases on next year's
   profits? What weaknesses in the business emerge from a study
   of the accounts reproduced here? What action do you think
   the chief executive should take on this evidence?
3. The chief executive has set targets for his subordinates in
   the same way as targets have been set for him. What sort of
   targets do you think he might have set? Give examples for a
   variety of his senior executives. How would you expect their
   performances to be monitored? How would you expect deviations
   in performance to be dealt with? Be as specific as possible.
4. Using the sales figures in Table 18.1 calculate the trend of
   sales and project this trend for the next two years.
5. To what extent do you think Billy MacDougall will be able to
   achieve the objectives set for him? What steps do you think
   he should take in the circumstances?

After discussing these topics with other members of the group,
play the role of a personal assistant and draft an appropriate
report to the chief executive.

19.   The Bank Manager — Role Play

One of the functions of a bank manager is to grant loans and/or
overdrafts to his customers. The usual arrangement is that a
particular branch manager is given a specific limit up to which
he can lend without security (or collateral) from his customer.
Any amounts above the limit generally need to be sanctioned by
the advances department at head office.

Brian Cox has recently been appointed manager at the Barbridge
branch of the Northern District Bank Ltd. It is one of the
smaller commercial banks and operates in the border counties
between England and Scotland. At the end of last week three
different customers came to him for financial support and he
has been considering their applications.

GRAHAM SQUIRES is a builder in his late thirties. He has taken
over the company started by his father in 1949 - C. Squires and
Sons Ltd. The company flourished in the period up to 1973, at
which time the father left the business to be run by his eldest
son, Graham. The method of operation has remained unchanged. The
company buys parcels of land, builds estates of houses and
sells them with the help of estate agents. Considerable sums of
capital are tied up in the operations and this creates cash flow
problems when sales are slow.

Graham is asking for an overdraft of up to £25,000 to meet
outstanding bills. He is offering as security the deeds of five
unsold properties in the latest estate of Squires-built houses.
The five properties offered as security are freehold and the
asking price for each is £23,000. They were completed just before
last Christmas. In the meantime the Squires workforce have been
engaged on sub-contract work building a block of offices in the
town centre. The company is owed £36,000 by Apex Ltd, the company
organising the building programme. Graham explained to Brian Cox
that he is expecting a cheque in settlement from Apex during the
course of the next few days. The bank manager, however, knows
that this is unlikely. Apex also bank at the Barbridge branch and
they are in dire straits financially. The developer for whom
they built the office block has failed to pay the last,
substantial instalment due and they have heard that a receiver
in bankruptcy is to be appointed. Brian has had a long session
with the financial director of Apex and although the bank is
a secured creditor, other creditors are not likely to be paid in
full. On the evidence available Brian reckons that Apex would be
able to pay about 30p in the pound to their creditors. Apex
have applied for a loan from the Northern District but it is

almost certain to be turned down by head office. It is with these thoughts in mind that the manager studies his customer's latest accounts (see Table 19.1).

TABLE 19.1   Balance sheet of C. Squires and Sons Ltd as at 31 December 198-

	(£)		(£)
Capital		Workshop and office	
80,000 ordinary shares		(at cost 1977)	30,000
of £1 each	80,000	Plant and equipment	
Reserves	38,350	less depreciation	4,351
Balance on profit and loss		Vehicles less	
account	867	depreciation	1,300
	————	Building land	
	119,217	(at cost 1981)	65,000
		Work in progress	82,472
Liabilities		Prepayments	180
Creditors	80,148	Debtors less provision	
Tax due	2,950	for bad debts	3,855
Accrued expenses	215	Materials (at cost)	11,109
	83,313	Balance at bank	4,105
		Cash in hand	158
	202,530		202,530

Notes:

1. Net profit for the year was £22,500; dividends paid on the shares have been a regular 12½% since 1970.
2. The shares are held by:

   Charles Squires (father) - 50,000;
   Leonard Squires (brother) - 5000. He is a partner in a local firm of solicitors and is not actively involved in the building business;
   Graham Squires - 25,000.

3. Present current account balances:

   (a) at Barbridge branch - C. Squires and Sons Ltd (£79.15 overdrawn)
                              Graham Squires (£2187.65)
   (b) at other Northern District branches
                            - Charles Squires (£2985.85)

4. The small workforce employed by Squires is presently employed building a new luxury bungalow for Charles Squires.

YOUR FIRST ASSIGNMENT (assuming group work is possible)
Choose two members of the group to play the roles of Brian Cox and Graham Squires. Let them play out the interview which might take place between the two men. The rest of the group can subsequently criticise the performances.

110

YOUR SECOND ASSIGNMENT
Draw up a list of twenty questions which you think Brian Cox
should have asked Graham Squires before submitting the application
to head office. Then write up a brief report (150-200 words)
such as the manager might send to his head office with the
overdraft application.

TERRY WOOD was employed by a large textile group as a research
chemist until eighteen months ago when he was made redundant as
the result of a plant closure. In his late fifties there was
little hope of re-employment and the future looked bleak.
However he used his redundancy pay to carry on a research project
literally in his own back garden. The result was the discovery
of an ingenious and comparatively inexpensive technique for
double-glazing windows. The process was demonstrated for Brian
Cox's predecessor when he was approached for funds originally.
He was convinced the idea deserved financial backing.
   The technique involves placing an 0.5 cm sheet of a specially
treated material on the existing window-pane. The material can
be cut easily to size. Once the material is fastened to the
glass (with a small amount of clear fixative), a chemical spray
is applied which has the effect of slowly evaporating the
treated material. The process of evaporation extends over a
period of twenty-four hours. Within minutes it is possible to
move to the final stage whereby a specially developed liquid
plastic is sprayed on to the evaporating material. The plastic
solidifies rapidly and provided the correct quantities are used
the solution crystallises into a wafer-thin sheet of clear
plastic. After twenty-four hours you have, in effect, the original
window-pane, an 0.5 cm vacuum and a thin but remarkably strong
inner window-pane. In total a very effective insulating device
and one which has an overwhelming advantage compared to existing
methods in that the cost of double-glazing is reduced by over
50%.
   The bank were not the only ones impressed with the new
technique. A national firm offering a double-glazing service
bought the patent from Terry Wood for a sum of £50,000 with the
avowed intent of introducing the device 'at a later date'. The
agreement allowed Terry to produce the kits for sales overseas
so long as they were not re-introduced into the United Kingdom
market.
   The Northern District Bank - through Brian's predecessor -
gave a substantial loan to Terry to enable him to set up the
production of kits and he decided, in the first place, to
concentrate sales in the Canadian market where he had some
contacts already. The business is proving very successful - so
successful that Terry needs a further injection of cash.
   Terry had used the money he received for the patent, plus the
loan from the bank (£35,000) to buy a seven-year lease for a
small factory on the outskirts of Barbridge. He has bought the
necessary machinery on hire purchase and taken on a total of
thirty-six workers.
   'I've got this firm in Canada who are buying the whole of my
output', Terry explained to the manager last week.' I just can't

produce enough for them. According to my accountant I'm making a fortune - but that's only on paper.'

Brian Cox had asked Terry to come and see him because he was anxious about the loan repayments. Terry had agreed to repay the £35,000 over a period of three years but at the end of the first year only £5000 had been repaid and then only at the expense of an increasing overdraft. To the manager's initial consternation Terry had turned the discussion round to a plea for more capital. His request was for a further £35,000 loan. He has even produced an amusing diagram (see Figure 19.1) for Brian showing just what his problem is.

FIGURE 19.1

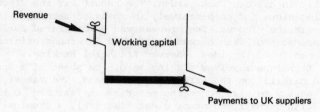

The manager realises that the basic problem here is one of 'over-trading'. A cash flow deficit may develop because a business is expanding rapidly. Raw materials are bought on, say, one month's credit. If there is a delay of more than one month between incurring the debt and receiving payment from the purchasers - as there obviously is in this case - there will be a shortage of working capital.

'I get nearly all my supplies from Jenson's,' the manager recalled Terry saying, 'and they give me a 2½% trade discount if I settle within a month.'

He was also rather pleased with the way the exchange rates had worked in his favour.

'I've even made a profit out of the currency', he had said proudly. 'Sterling improved against the dollar at just the right time.'

His bank manager was less happy about the situation. He made a note on his working papers. He also studied the accounts (Tables 19.2 and 19.3) which had been prepared by Terry's accountant up to the end of last month.

TABLE 19.2   Draft profit and loss account for past six months*

	(£)	(£)		(£)	(£)
Stock (at			Net sales	(85,764)	110.641
start)	–	13,244	Profit on currency		
Net purchases	(22,550)	23,975	exchanges		3,234
	(22,550)	37,219			
Stock (at					
end)	(13,244)	11,129			
	(9,306)	26,090			
Wages	(58,008)	61,656			
Carriage	(2,050)	3,049			
Electricity	(863)	1,292			
Rates	(752)	752			
Bank charges	(2,513)	2,856			
Depreciation	(807)	1,937			
General					
expenses	(105)	167			
Net profit					
c/d	(11,360)	16,076			
	(85,764)	113,875		(85,764)	113,875

* Results for previous six months in brackets.

TABLE 19.3   Balance sheet as at end of last month*

	(£)	(£)		(£)	(£)
Capital	(40,000)	46,360	Cash in hand	(121)	135
add net					
profit	(11,360)	16,070	Bank balance	(2,587)	–
	(51,360)	62,430	Stocks	(11,295)	11,129
less					
drawings	(8,000)	10,000	Debtors	(51,432)	69,378
	(43,360)	52,430	Equipment less		
			depreciation	(30,696)	28,759
Bank loan	(33,000)	30,000	Leasehold		
Accrued			property	(25,000)	25,000
interest	(375)	625			
Bank					
overdraft	–	3,117			
Creditors	(44,396)	48,229			
	(121,131)	134,401		(121,131)	134,401

YOUR THIRD ASSIGNMENT
What advice would you give to Terry Wood, if you were in the
bank manager's shoes? And what sort of report would you put
forward to head office to accompany your customer's application
for further funds?

JOANNA PEEL is the only child of a highly respected local doctor. She loves horses, and when she left school two years ago her father bought her a riding school a few miles out of Barbridge. Although the school seems to be quite popular the business could hardly be regarded as a money-spinner according to Joanna's current account. It is overdrawn by £82.15 at the present time and the average balance over the past twelve months has only been £100. She has recently drawn two cheques in settlement of bills for animal fodder which had to be returned 'post-dated' - in each case they were dated one week ahead and Joanna was obviously trying to delay the payments.

She is now seeking a loan of £4000 to purchase a second-hand Land Rover and horse-box. She has explained to the bank manager that some of her pupils have been very successful in local gymkhanas and the new transport would help them to compete further afield. Brian Cox wished her business acumen would match her riding skills. He had asked for the latest accounts of the riding school and she shrugged her shoulders.

'I'll have to get an accountant to have a look at things for me but I just haven't got round to it yet. I've just been too busy', she had said.

But on the subject of collaterals (security) she had been more helpful. When her mother had died she had inherited some securities in a family business - Garfield Stores Ltd. So she was able to offer as security *either* 10,000 £1 ordinary stock units *or* £10,000 8½% redeemable mortgage debentures.

The company is a public one but its shares are not quoted on a stock exchange. The manager has been able to confirm that the company has paid dividends of 40% gross regularly over the last six years. He also knows that the debentures are redeemable at the end of next year.

YOUR FINAL ASSIGNMENT
Again standing in the shoes of the bank manager, answer the following questions:

1. How would you deal with Joanna's application for an advance?
2. What specific advice would you offer this young lady?
3. What are the detractions of a security which does not have a stock exchange quotation?
4. Which of the securities would you prefer, and why?
5. Why would you be annoyed when Joanna draws post-dated cheques?
6. What risks would be run if the customer's cheques were at some time sent back to the presenter with the notation 'Refer to drawer' or 'Insufficient funds'?
7. What personal qualities, if any, would you look for in a customer to whom you were lending money?

20. The Twilight Village

The idea came to Dai Williams high up over the Atlantic on the
return trip from New York to Gatwick. He had gone to the United
States to look at a new building material which had been
developed, which was reckoned to be both cheaper and more durable
than anything else currently available on the market. Dai is the
Managing Director and Chairman of Tregaron Property Developments
CCC.* His father had set up the company over fifty years ago and
originally the *modus operandi* had been to buy up small plots of
land in North Wales and Cheshire, build a couple of houses or
cottages and then move on to the next site. Operations are very
different now, however. The company still build houses but they
build them in large estates and they build them all over the
north of England. They have also involved themselves in the
construction of a number of office blocks on the outskirts of
Manchester. These blocks have been leased to a variety of
insurance companies and property groups.

While in the US he had been invited to visit his Aunt Gwynneth
who had married a USAAF sergeant in the Second World War and had
lived in Bangor, Maine for most of the intervening years.
However she was recently widowed and being frail and elderly,
sold up her home and moved down to what might be described as a
colony of retired people in South Carolina. He had only been able
to spend a weekend with her but he was greatly impressed with
what he saw.

Some 220 cabins (as they called them) had been built in
clusters of five or six. The whole area had been skilfully
landscaped so that it was pleasant in appearance while optimally
convenient for the elderly inhabitants. The cabins were close
together and compact in design. They were provided with all sorts
of labour-saving devices as well as a range of services which
included a mobile laundry and a luxury 'meals on wheels'
arrangement. There was also a centrally situated social activities
centre which was used for a variety of functions including film
shows and social gatherings.

Keeping a watchful eye on the well-being of the elderly folk
were a small team of aides. They were young and wore distinctive
outfits, but each of them had some special qualification which
enabled them to serve the community. According to Aunt Gwynneth
most of the females were trained nurses while their partners

* A public company registered in Wales may substitute CCC for Plc,
  those initials in Welsh standing for *Cwmni Cyfyngedig Cyhoeddus*
  (Public Limited Company).

included a taxi driver and a chiropodist. Dai was amused to hear the aides described as PCs (short for 'problem-copers'). Apparently the old folk contracted for these services when they purchased their cabins either paying a lump sum for perpetuity or agreeing to pay a fixed sum annually. It became obvious that the project was not aimed at the poorer section of the community when Aunt Gwynneth told her nephew she had paid out a total of $100,000 for her new home. But as she explained, 'I haven't got any children I can turn to and this is a darn sight better than the usual home for geriatrics.'

Dai made a few simple sketches (see Figure 20.1) to remind him of what he had seen. Each of the cabins has a linked shower cubicle and washroom, but as the siting of these varies he has excluded them from his sketch. He had started out on his trip looking for some new and more effective material for building office blocks but instead his mind was turning to what might be done to provide an idyllic setting for old people in the UK. His imagination was fanned by the realisation that the proportion of old people was growing steadily – a growth industry if ever there was one!

FIGURE 20.1

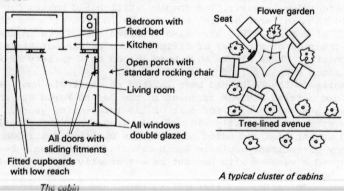

Bedroom with fixed bed
Kitchen
Open porch with standard rocking chair
Living room
All windows double glazed
All doors with sliding fitments
Fitted cupboards with low reach
The cabin

Flower garden
Seat
Tree-lined avenue
A typical cluster of cabins

Dai's motives are not entirely philanthropic. He is first and foremost a businessman. But he sees no reason why philanthropy and commerce should not be bedfellows. When he got back to his office he started a serious investigation into the possibilities of duplicating the South Carolina retirement colony in his native Wales. Of course he appreciated that some modifications would be necessary. One of the biggest problems he knew would be finding a suitable tract of land for such a development. Building land was increasingly scarce and expensive. The only suitable land on offer was a 2½ acre plot on the outskirts of a west coast seaside town and the asking price was £200,000 an acre.

Just when he was giving up hope of getting the project off the ground one of his co-directors mentioned at a board lunch that a small but well-known holiday camp in North Wales was rumoured to be running into cash flow problems. It was of no more than passing interest but later in the day Dai got round to thinking about some of the possibilities. He asked his personal assistant to obtain a copy of the holiday camp's accounts and asked his

TABLE 20.1   Balance sheet of Snowdonia Holiday Camps Ltd (a private company) as at December 31 last

	At Dec. 31 last	At Dec. 31 previous year		At Dec. 31 last	At Dec. 31 previous year
	(£)	(£)		(£)	(£)
Ordinary stock (units of 25p)	600,000	600,000	Land at 1975 valuation	970,000	970,000
General reserves	189,976	189,976	Buildings at cost:	49,118	52,382
	789,976	789,976	less depreciation		
Sundry creditors	36,485	19,051	Stock and equipment	46,307	47,410
Bank loan	212,765	225,582	less depreciation		
Bank overdraft	24,325	5,431	Sundry debtors	5,124	6,329
Outstanding taxation	7,450	32,892	Cash	1,247	2,152
Balance on profit and loss account	795	5,341			
	1,071,796	1,078,273		1,071,796	1,078,273

Other data:

	Year to Dec. 31 last	For previous year	Average over last 5 years
Profits/losses	£3,867 loss	£32,742 profit	£98,887 profit
Ordinary divs	nil	5%	12.5%

Dai has added a note for Ruth to the effect that his personal valuation of the land and buildings owned by Snowdonia is as follows:

	Coastal site	Inland site
Land	£600,000	£1,000,000
At replacement cost:		
Supermarket	90,000	120,000
Restaurant	180,000	195,000

stockbroker for some information about the company. The information that he received is shown in Table 20.1.

In the meantime he visited the site of the camps owned by the company. He made a few vital notes on what he discovered on his visits. These are given below, as he wrote them up.

Coastal site: approx. 4 acres - 63 timber-clad one-room chalets - estimated life ten years - each contains 2/4 bunks - hanging space for clothes - washing but no cooking facilities - communal restaurant - excellent kitchens - small supermarket - brick - built two years ago - camp run by 3 permanent staff - 18 part-timers employed during summer season (first week of June to first week of September inclusive) - the more popular of the two sites.

Inland site: approx. $10\frac{1}{2}$ acres - 8 miles from Coastal Site - $1\frac{1}{2}$ miles from the sea - 212 chalets - many in poor condition - similar services to those at coastal site but buildings older and in poor repair - $1\frac{1}{2}$ acres have been set apart for caravanners and campers - 15 permanent staff (including office and booking clerks) - augmented by 26 part-timers in the season - mainly female.

Basing his ideas on the South Carolina colony Dai estimates that he would be able to build a cluster of five cabins on about 0.4 acres.

Dai's plans are clear-cut in his mind but he values the advice of his young Personal Assistant, Ruth Davies. He explains the project to her and provides her with the same information you have been given here.

'I'd like a brief report', he says. 'I want to know what you see as the options. I'd like to know how you evaluate them. By all means let me have your recommendations but these are not the vital part of the report. I want to put my ideas to the board at the end of next week and I don't want to overlook any bright ideas or practical problems that you can anticipate. Obviously one of the options is a takeover bid for Snowdonia Holiday Camps. What price do you think we should be prepared to pay on the evidence we've got? What snags are there likely to be? I reckon to spend £25,000 on labour and materials for each of the cabins with a further £150,000 on what I call environmental expenditure - a shop and a community centre and so on.'

Ruth bit the end of her pen. The more capable she proved to be the more challenging the tasks her boss gave her. That was as it should be. At least Dai Williams did not under-rate her capabilities.

YOUR ASSIGNMENT
Prepare a report on the lines you feel Ruth might have submitted it to Dai Williams. The only other data she obtains is the latest set of accounts from Tregaron Property (shown in Table 20.2).

TABLE 20.2   Tregaron Property Developments CCC

(a) *Profit and loss account*

	Year to 30 June last	Previous year
	(£000s)	(£000s)
Turnover: construction	1,615	1,895
rents	521	316
Trading profit: construction	219	203
rents	417	418
Total trading profit	636	621
Interest payable (net)	73	73
	563	548
Taxation	31	29
Profits after taxation	532	519
Dividends	260	260
Profits retained	272	259

(b) *Balance sheet*

		At 30 June last		At 30 June previous year
		(£000s)		(£000s)
Net assets employed				
Land and buildings		5,000		5,000
Other fixed assets		450		436
Goodwill		100		120
Stock exchange investments (market value 30 June)		660		430
Current assets Debtors	48		78	
Work in progress	198		154	
Stock	76		68	
Cash	70	392	12	312
Total assets		6,602		6,298
Less current liabilities		244		171
		£6,358		£6,127
Financed by				
Ordinary stock (£1 units)		1,500		1,500
7½% preference stock (£1 units)		800		800
Reserves		3,000		2,741
Loan capital		1,000		1,000
Deferred taxation		58		86
		£6,358		£6,127

QUESTIONS FOR GROUP DISCUSSION
Do you think aging members of society should be cared for by
the state? By their families? Or should they look after
themselves? To the extent that finance is required where do you
think it should come from? What are the merits of takeovers such
as Dai Williams is contemplating here from an economic viewpoint?
And the demerits?

21. The French Connection

Mooney's Mail Order House has been in business for the past
twenty years. Customers are sent a glossy catalogue twice a year
displaying a range of goods including clothing for the whole
family, furniture for every room in the house, consumer durables
of all types, jewellery, sports goods, gardening requisites and
toys, etc. The appeal of this form of selling is that the
customers do not need to leave their homes to do their shopping.
No deposit is required on the purchase and payment can be
spread over twenty weeks or longer in the case of more expensive
purchases. No interest is payable during this period of credit.
A further feature is that account holders/agents are given a 10%
commission on the sale of goods over the total value of £100 in
any calendar year. It is intended that office and factory workers
will show the catalogue to their workmates and that housewives
will do the same to their friends and neighbours.

La Mode Parisienne is a broadly similar business operating in
northern France and Belgium. It also sells through the medium of
a glossy catalogue but there are some distinguishing features
compared to the British set-up. The French mail order firm
concentrates almost exclusively on the sale of clothes, and tends
to be up-market compared to its British counterpart and does not
offer commission to agents.

Joel Beldray, who is the Managing Director and principal
shareholder in Mooney's Mail Order Ltd (he owns 55% of the voting
shares), has recently been in contact with Jean-Paul Puisset,
a Director and major shareholder in the French company (he owns
30% of the equity). The proposal is that each company should
acquire a 40% holding in the equity of the other and that Beldray
would become a director in the French company while Puisset would
join the Mooney board. From Beldray's point of view the purpose
of this tie-in is threefold:

(1) to halt the decline in sales of fashion clothes in the Mooney
    enterprise - sales have declined by 22% over the past three
    years;
(2) to acquire a springboard for sales of Mooney's wide range of
    goods into Europe, taking France as the first stop;
(3) to use a 3 million franc loan provided by Puisset personally
    to develop a series of one-hour video tapes in which clothing
    offered for sale in catalogues is also displayed by live
    models with a musical accompaniment (disco style).

The idea is that customers receiving the catalogues will be
offered video tapes for a refundable hiring fee. They will be

able to see the clothes modelled and refer to the catalogue for further details. There will be varied backgrounds so that items other than clothing will receive exposure. For example, swimwear will be modelled with a background of tenting equipment, summer dresses with sporting or gardening equipment, and so on..It is accepted that Puisset's company will benefit most through the sale of La Mode Parisienne garments which will take over from most of the existing Mooney ranges. But Mooney's will hope to share in these profits both from the mark-up on the French dresses and the 40% share in the equity of the French company. Furthermore, they hope to benefit from the reciprocal arrangement whereby a Mooney warehouse is set up on the outskirts of Paris to supply French customers with kitchen furniture, etc., sold through the enlarged La Mode Parisienne catalogue together with the video cassettes. Of course one item which Mooney's expect to sell well as a result of the tying-in of the companies is the video cassette recorder, which will be essential if the video cassettes are to be played.

As attractive as these ideas might sound they are meeting a considerable amount of opposition. At boardroom level Marjorie Staples, Joel's sister, who owns 15% of the voting shares, complains that the proposed link-up between the French and British companies will give all the advantages to the French firm.

'It's just a way of finding an outlet for their dresses in England', she says. 'That's why Puisset is prepared to give us the loan.' Her main concern is that the French company make up the dresses they sell and therefore stand to benefit most.

The comments of the remaining directors and the senior executives indicate varying degrees of enthusiasm for the project.

NORMAN HATHAWAY (a non-executive director who holds 8% of the voting shares and 60% of the preference shares): I agree with Marjorie. I don't see any advantage in putting ourselves at the mercy of this fellow Puisset. What happens if he demands repayment of the loan?

EDMUND HORLOCK (Financial Director holding 8% of the voting shares and 40% of the preference shares): We know how much this video cassette project is going to cost. What we don't know is how much cash flow is going to be generated. I also want to know how much Puisset is going to pay for our shares, and how much we're going to pay for his. When I know that I'll tell you what I think of this plan.

ROGER PURVIS (a non-executive director who holds 4% of the voting shares): It sounds a great idea.

JOHN FARNES (Catalogue Editor): Who's going to decide on what goes into our catalogues in future? I can see us producing a joint catalogue. Is it going to be in French *and* English? I can see problems! Half of my work at least is going to disappear!

CAROL THRACE (Chief Fashion Buyer): Our customers want English clothes. Housewives in Barnsley wouldn't want haute couture even if they could afford it. Fancy clothes - fancy prices!

JANE COLLINGE (Personnel Manager): We haven't got a single person on our staff who can speak French!

Carol Thrace has also produced some statistics to show how

dependent Mooney's are on the sale of dresses and ladies' wear generally. The figures shown in Table 21.1 are from a recent computer printout.

TABLE 21.1   Cumulative totals for last six months

	Sales	Returns	Net
	(£)	(£)	(£)
Ladies' wear – fashion	612173.62	103207.52	508966.10
coats	58374.69	11279.46	47095.23
other	69974.52	6155.29	63819.23
Mens' wear – suits	19846.56	3024.56	16822.00
other	53219.17	1835.78	51383.39
Childrens' wear	11346.75	1109.65	10237.10
Footwear	14382.32	1711.19	12671.13
Audio visual entertainment	149562.88	6712.34	142850.54
Cameras and accessories	12365.12	108.26	12256.86
Car accessories	21198.58	187.56	21011.02
Electrical goods	323944.40	16112.86	307831.54
Furnishings	36648.05	811.40	35836.65
Furniture	171346.18	2555.19	168790.99
Gardening equipment	9980.01	105.00	9875.01
Hardware	71009.56	2036.78	68972.78
Sports	5614.39	83.88	5530.51
Toys	122892.07	1005.63	121886.44
Watches and jewellery	28712.82	3885.87	24826.95
Miscellaneous	19913.57	806.24	19107.33
Totals	1812505.26	162734.46	1649770.80

One of the criticisms of the proposal for introducing video cassettes is that only one in ten households have playback facilities at the present time – according to Bill Freeman, the Marketing Manager – but he has produced an insert for the catalogue when the new service is introduced (see below). He is hoping to make a deal with one of the manufacturers of video cassette decks which will allow the machines to be offered at an especially low price. From past experience he expects them to bring down the price to 50% of the list price which will leave Mooney's with the problem of deciding how much of the benefit to pass on to their customers.

An Invitation

Mooney's are proud to offer their customers an incredible double to start off the new season. Our pièce de résistance is the introduction of **haute couture from the famous French** Fashion House of La Mode Parisienne. We are offering the most elegant clothes at the most reasonable prices. High fashion at rock bottom prices. And it is not only the women we are catering for. Have a look at some of the new styles for men. Panache at a price everyone can afford! Here are **clothes** with a difference. The cut is superior, the material is finer, the style is unmistakably French. Only the price reminds you that you are dealing with Mooney's. We always make sure that you are not paying one penny more than you need for anything you buy from our catalogue. Do not take our word for it. See for yourself! And that is where we introduce our second surprise.

Until now our customers have had to browse through our catalogue to see the wonderful bargains we offer. Not that browsing through our catalogue is any sort of hardship. But we are now offering you the opportunity to watch a parade of our products on the screens of your televisions. With one of our special video cassettes you will be able to look in on our new disco boutique and see the models actually walking **around** in those lovely French lawn cotton dresses. You will be able to see the effect that it has on a rather ordinary phlegmatic Englishman when he dons the garb of those knowing French.

And the cost of this new video service? Nothing. Absolutely nothing. If you want to teleview these wonderful fashions all you have to do is to complete the order form below. We will then send you the first of the video cassettes (there are three in all). We will charge your account with the sum of £5 but this amount will be credited to your account in full when you return the video cassette to us — after you have had a chance to see whether our boast is justified or not. We claim to have on offer the best bargains in the land!

Of course you need a video cassette recorder to play back our new fashion cassettes and we can even help you to acquire this vital piece of equipment. Mooney's have made a bulk purchase of video cassette recorders from the country's leading manufacturer. These recorders are offered to you at an unrepeatable price (see page ... of the catalogue for details). You might even find a way of making the recorder pay for itself. We suggest many of your friends would like to see our fashions in motion-videos. Why not view them together? Invite them round for a coffee and let them look at the wonderful bargains and stand by for a rush of orders. All you have to do is to complete one of the special yellow Video Party order forms and we will give you a special 5% commission in addition to your normal 10% agency commission.

Whether or not you avail yourself of these opportunities you will find our pictorial catalogue makes interesting reading. It provides the bargain hunter with the usual crop of bargains. Good hunting!.

Daniel Mackintosh
Marketing Manager

QUESTIONS TO BE ANSWERED

1. What criticisms would you offer in relation to the marketing director's message to Mooney's customers? What changes would you make?

2. What problems would Joel Beldray face in imposing his views on his fellow directors? How do you think he might overcome the resistance? To what extent do you think the resistance is justified?

3. How would you account for the lack of enthusiasm for the new project on the part of the senior executives? How do you think this problem might be coped with by the chief executive?

4. How would you display the statistics in Table 21.1 diagramatically? Consider alternative forms and decide which would be most helpful.

5. Bearing in mind the statistics provided by the financial director (see Table 21.2), what would you regard as an

equitable arrangement for the exchange of shares between
Mooney's and La Mode Parisienne?

TABLE 21.2   Abridged balance sheets as at 30 September 198-

	Mooney's Mail Order Ltd (£s thous.)		La Mode Parisienne S.A. (francs thous.)
Fixed assets			
Premises		772	5,950
Capital equipment less depreciation		103	2,517
Goodwill		200	
		1,075	8,467
Current assets			
Stocks		405	3,808
Work in progress			612
Debtors	1,843		12,577
Less bad debt provision	92	1,751	
Cash at bank			311
		2,156	17,308
Total assets		3,231	25,775
Less current liabilities			
Bank overdraft	89		
Creditors	1,059	1,148	2,013
		2,083	23,762
Financed by			
Ordinary shares (£1)		1,000 (100 francs)	18,000
7½% preference shares (£1 each)		500	
Reserves		98	5,762
		1,598	23,762
12% mortgage debentures		400	
Deferred taxation		85	
		2,083	23,762

Profits after taxation (average over last 5 years):
Mooney's Mail Order Ltd   £223,425
La Mode Parisienne   3.6m francs

Ordinary dividends:
Mooney's ordinary dividend was a regular 15% until 1980. Since
then the dividend has been reduced to 5% per annum. La Mode
Parisienne has paid a regular 10% per annum to its equity owners
since its incorporation in 1970.

22. Joint Consultation — Group Role Playing

Peter Roach founded the business in his native Nottingham over fifty years ago. He was a master baker and used to take his wares to the various markets in the East Midlands. In the early days he would load his van with bread and cakes and take his family with him to work in the stalls at the market places. His business expanded largely as a result of his talent for making fancy cakes and he began to supply his products to shops and restaurants throughout the East Midlands. A limited liability company was incorporated in 1961 and a few years later the company went public. One of the larger insurance companies purchased a substantial number of the new ordinary shares and they still hold 30% of the equity. The insurance company make no attempt to interfere with the running of the company and so Peter's son Robert, with 20% of the ordinary shares (carrying one vote each) is able to exercise full control. However the insurance company are now suggesting the time might be ripe for applying for a quotation on the London Stock Exchange. They link this with the need to widen the range of products.

Following his father's death in 1971, Robert Roach enlarged the bakeries and concentrated production on three best-selling lines:

Tango Bars: chocolate biscuits with fruit-flavoured centres - there is a choice of seven different flavours.
Quartet Mini-cakes: packed in boxes of six, with a variety of shapes and flavours.
Mother Made fruit cakes.

Robert Roach accepts that the success of his products has been founded on slick advertising and attractive presentation. A valuable contract to supply one of the country's largest super-market chains has provided an assured level of sales though this particular contract is dependent on regular and unbroken deliveries. This is why industrial relations are so vital at the Roach works. The excellent record to date is ascribed to the efficacy of the joint consultation committee which was set up ten years ago. 80% of the workforce belong to a union: the break-down is shown in Table 22.1.

There are 27 shop stewards representing the workforce. The essential qualification for shop stewards is that they must be members of one of the three unions. They are elected by ballot by all union members in a particular section. None of the sales or administration staff (27 men and 71 women) belong to a union. The shop stewards have elected seven of their number, including

TABLE 22.1

	Non-union	Bakers' Union	Transport and General Workers' Union	Amalgamated Union of Engineering Workers
Men	27	712	63	36
Women	254	12	296	0
	281	724	359	36

the chief shop steward, to serve on the joint consultation committee which meets at 3 p.m. on the first Friday in every month, in the same committee room in which the board of directors meet. The chief shop steward and three other worker representatives on the committee are members of the Bakers Union. Two committee members belong to the TGWU while the remaining member carries an AUEW card. The strength of the Bakers Union generally at the Roach works is explained by the early history of the business.

The management team on the committee consists of Robert Roach as chief executive, the works manager, the personnel manager – the lone female on the committee – and the welfare officer. The chief executive is designated as chairman of the committee but is seldom able to attend, in which case the works manager deputises for him.

YOUR ASSIGNMENT
You are invited to assume the roles of those on the joint consultation committee and to cope with the problems confronting them at a meeting where the following items are included on the agenda. Background information is given to set out the salient features of each of the problems.

1. One of the problems facing employees at the Roach works is that the factory is in a built-up area and car-parking space is therefore limited. A new car park is in course of preparation and is designed to accommodate an additional 86 vehicles bringing the total capacity at the works to 390. The present allocation is as follows:

Visitors	Senior executives	Sales and admin.	Foremen and supervisors	Other staff	Total
12	8	32	112	140	304

The present system is that numbered car-parking discs are provided by the chief timekeeper. Car-parking space is regarded as one of the perks of certain supervisory/managerial posts. The remaining spaces are allocated to the longest-serving members of staff applying. Irritation has been caused because (i) some employees do not always use their spaces and (ii) there have been instances reported when those with spaces allocated have made a charge for the use of the space by others. The committee decided at their last meeting to reconsider the whole question of parking spaces now that the new park is about to become operational. Certain ideas have already been proposed.

(a) Spaces might be allocated to the different divisions/departments according to the number of personnel in each. Each department would then decide how the distribution should be effected (see Table 22.2).

(b) A rental might be charged with the money raised going to the staff social fund, which is used to support activities such as bingo, football and amateur dramatics.
(c) Spaces might be allocated monthly by lot.

TABLE 22.2   Analysis of workforce by department and status

Grade	Sales and admin.	Tango line 1	Tango line 2	Quartet line	Mother Made	Stores and dispatch	Packing
1.	59	297	276	286	181	127*	112
2.	29	33	32	32	27	17	19
3.	13	3	3	3	2	2	3

* includes driver/roundsmen
Grade 3 = managers; Grade 2 = foremen/supervisors; Grade 1 = others.

2. Some of the machinery and equipment is over twenty years old and the company is desirous of introducing new equipment as soon as possible. The plan is to have a section of the *Quartet* production line fully automated. Although the company is market leader in the small fancy pastry range, it is felt that the new production line will help to stabilise costs and counter increasing pressure from competitors.

The new robot equipment will reduce the workforce required on the *Quartet* line by 80% and it has to be decided how to cope with this problem. There has already been discussion - at last month's meeting - and management has indicated that labour turnover is running at around 14% per annum in the company generally. The company is willing to stop recruiting for six months to allow natural wastage to take its effect, but some workers will still need to be made redundant. The JCC is looking for a formula by means of which staff may be selected for dismissal. The ideas which have been proposed to date include:

(a) A reduction in working hours. The workers are currently working 38 hours per week. This should be reduced to 36 hours but the hourly wage rates should not be changed.
(b) Workers should be selected for redundancy on a last in, first out basis.
(c) Those with the least satisfactory attendance records and performance should be dismissed first.
(d) Females with husbands who have jobs, either in the Roach company or elsewhere should be invited to retire voluntarily.
(e) Employees over the age of 55 should be retired early. There

are 74 people in this age group (43 of them are foremen, supervisors or managers).

3. Under a recent national pay agreement all weekly paid workers at Roach were awarded a flat increase of 28p per hour. The problem is that the company's job evaluation scheme has given the maintenance engineers a positive differential of approximately 25% and the AUEW shop stewards are now claiming that this award needs to be adjusted for their members in order to restore the differential previously acknowledged as their due and based largely on their special skills and qualifications. The TGWU stewards are in dispute with the engineers on this issue, claiming that the narrowing of the gap in pay makes up in part for a failure of the job evaluation scheme to account for the extremely boring nature of much of the work undertaken by their members. Management has agreed to restore the differential to the extent of an additional 10p per hour to be paid to the maintenance engineers - so long as this does not lead to a leap-frogging situation where the acceptance of the engineers' claim will activate a parity claim by the TGWU members, followed by a further claim from the engineers for a restoration of the differential.

   While the Bakers Union shop stewards have not so far made their views known they are very much involved because some 15% of their members enjoy various degrees of advantage under the job evaluation scheme. The points awarded to their members are largely to cover unsocial hours. An early and late shift are in operation in the bakery section of the production lines. The problem for the Bakers Union representatives is that the majority of their members are in agreement with the TGWU on this issue.

4. In the fruit-pulping section of the *Tango* production lines the majority of workers are of West Indian extraction. This is not as a result of any selection policy on the part of management. Rather it is because the atmosphere is very cheerful in this particular section and the existing employees have tended to encourage their friends to join them. A problem has now emerged in that a young white recruit who joined the section a month ago has been found distributing racist literature in the works. Unanimously, the remaining men - there are no women in this section - have given notice that they refuse to work with him though they will delay taking action until the outcome of this committee meeting is known.

   The young man who has caused the problem has joined the TGWU and has made it known that any discrimination against him will be referred to the Race Relations Board. It is clear that he would welcome publicity for his cause.

   The company workforce is multi-racial and to date this has not created problems. Some views have already been expressed by the workers' representatives on the JCC ranging from 'The company should sack him' and 'Give him the dirtiest jobs - he'll soon leave', to 'Transfer him to another section' and even 'It's a free country'.

When Robert Roach heard of the trouble he sent a brief
memorandum to his personnel manager which read as follows:

MEMORANDUM

To Mrs Kate Marshall   From Robert Roach
   Personnel Manager   Chief Executive

I am sorry I shall not be able to get to the JCC meeting
tomorrow afternoon but I have heard about the trouble in the
fruit-pulping section. Will you make sure that this situation is
not over-dramatised. Our job is to make and sell cakes and
biscuits. We've got enough troubles on our hands. Play it cool.

PS It's a pity we ever took on this fellow.

---

23. Marsden Mini-Racers

The Marsden Motor Works is sited on the outskirts of an industrial
town in the Central Lowlands of Scotland. The payroll lists 680
employees, 30% of whom are women. The factory produces a variety
of specialised vehicles for the leisure industry, the most
important of which is the *Meteor* miniature racing car for use in
pleasure parks. The main attraction of the *Meteor* is the
electrically powered motor which keeps running costs to a minimum
and provides sufficient power to give the car a maximum speed of
30 kilometres per hour. The body is made of sectionalised
fibre-glass which makes for cheaper repairs and reconstructions.
The second biggest selling line for Marsden is the *Dodo* dodgem
car designed for use in fairgrounds.

The company has managed to take a substantial share of the
European market against strong opposition from an Italian
subsidiary of a major car company and a specialist German firm.
It is with the mounting competition in mind that Marsdens have
developed a Mark II version of the *Meteor* with a slightly more
powerful engine and an updated design which it is hoped will make
it more suitable for a new form of serious small-circuit racing –
hopefully persuading older/adult drivers to take part. Paul
Marsden, the Sales Director, is convinced that the development
of a new sport based on mini-racing cars is both feasible and one
of the best options available to them to combat an otherwise
shrinking and fiercely contested market. Some basic details of
sales and production over recent years are provided in
Table 23.1.

A prototype of the *Meteor Mark II* has been built and has
undergone extensive trials. The programme was delayed for a
vital six months when the chief designer left to take up an
appointment with one of the major car firms in the UK. However
the new model was eventually developed and a cheaper type of
fibre-glass is being used (having approximately 80% of the
strength of the material currently incorporated). It is
recognised that the frames will not stand up to heavy crashes,
but a compensatory factor is the hopefully lucrative market in
the provision of spares.

At the most recent meeting of the board of directors a
variety of information was presented (see Tables 23.2-7). Among
the topics discussed were:

1. The Italian competitors are known to have started production
   on a new model of the *Contessa* which will be 40 cm shorter
   and enjoy a $7\frac{1}{2}$% economy in petrol consumption without any
   deterioration in performance. Information is also available

TABLE 23.1   Sales over last four years and five months

	Meteors	Dodoes	Miscellaneous productions	Repairs and reconstructions*
This year to date:	(£)	(£)	(£)	(£)
May	93,137	105,298	43,287	205,864
April	201,703	100,362	46,918	186,319
March	198,366	98,537	33,744	102,514
February	160,732	90,672	30,017	86,694
January	183,581	87,469	28,629	95,718
Last year	2,486,599	1,700,163	512,434	1,824,419
Year 3	2,517,204	1,695,385	298,625	1,411,525
Year 2	2,398,165	2,037,466	309,918	1,095,123
Year 1	1,765,733	1,811,989	719,037	1,387,607
EXPORTS				
Germany				
Last year	185,292	100,474	15,726	62,894
Year 3	180,744	100,205	17,707	61,752
Year 2	172,606	98,918	13,606	60,795
Year 1	165,918	96,549	10,498	52,363
France				
Last year	212,538	115,601	9,348	100,712
Year 3	202,776	112,314	9,005	90,509
Year 2	200,891	108,790	8,787	81,316
Year 1	185,603	102,408	8,563	72,222
Netherlands				
Last year	159,672	32,605	15,862	23,763
Year 3	304,842	15,219	14,104	7,684
Year 2	271,719	7,909	12,950	2,205
Year 1	242,808	7,116	10,989	1,714
Belgium				
Last year	108,232	41,346	28,429	29,319
Year 3	132,607	38,611	25,363	28,056
Year 2	119,041	27,566	22,919	25,091
Year 1	108,636	19,435	18,808	22,202
Italy				
Last year	32,209	6,115	7,284	–
Year 3	33,016	3,017	5,815	–
Year 2	80,107	18,984	4,906	–
Year 1	93,051	2,506	3,872	–
Other countries				
Last year	194,509	112,015	21,316	–
Year 3	163,918	91,629	38,300	–
Year 2	140,076	60,334	3,850	–
Year 1	122,514	38,617	–	–

* Agents have been appointed to provide a reconstruction and repair service for *Meteor* owners in France, Belgium and the Netherlands. The revenue shown here includes the commissions receivable.

that purchasers of the new model will be given a two-year
term of credit before payment becomes due. Marsdens are
considering countering with an offer of credit terms
amounting to five equal payments over a period of two years.
2. A verbal report from Andy MacLellan, the Production Manager,
   blames a recent wave of one-day stoppages on a few militants
   who have been elected to the shop stewards' committee.
   Industrial relations have always been relatively commendable
   but during the last seven months a total of 3968 working
   days have been lost as a result of wildcat strikes. MacLellan
   is particularly incensed because the company acceded to union
   pressure to accept the principle of the closed shop. There are
   five different unions involved.
3. The need for finance to set up a new production line for the
   Meteor II. It has been intimated that some £500,000 will be
   required for the setting up of the new production line. It
   will be sited in the existing factory and plans are already
   well advanced. The appropriate high-technology equipment
   (robotic) has been tested on site and a provisional order
   has been placed.
4. The Financial Director, Angus Marsden, responded to a request
   at a previous meeting to comment on the possibility of taking
   advantage of the savings-related share option schemes referred
   to in the Finance Act 1980. He had looked at the appropriate
   sections in the Act and was of the opinion that the idea was
   not appropriate for Marsdens.

Company history
Fergus Marsden was born in the Gorbals district of Glasgow at the
turn of the century. It had been difficult to find regular work
from the beginning and when he married Kate and found himself
with a family to feed he was finally obliged to cross the border
to England to search for work. He found occasional employment on
fairgrounds and it was at this time he became interested in the
various mechanical apparatuses which were beginning to be associated
with them.

It was not until 1934 he finally found regular employment
repairing the small cars and dodgems which were beginning to
appear on some of the more sophisticated fairgrounds. He began to
trade in second-hand vehicles with some success. In 1937 he
acquired a long lease on a plot of land at the centre of a south
coast resort. With help from his bank manager he converted this
into a pleasure park, the central feature being a miniature race
track on which youngsters (often with one of their parents
alongside them) were able to race their cars around an oval track
for a few pence a circuit. Until the outbreak of war in 1939
Fergus prospered as never before, but when war came the resort
became a restricted area and his pleasure park was closed down.

However at the end of the war he was able to sell what was
left of his lease and used the proceeds to join forces with a
fellow Scot who was in the process of setting up a number of
holiday camps in Scotland and the north of England. Fergus
contracted to provide the various equipment required on the
associated pleasure parks. It was at this time that Marsden

Motors Ltd was incorporated, with Fergus as the owner of all but one of the shares. The company was very successful and extended its activities to the point where it was market leader for certain lines of fairground equipment. In the late 1970s though, the worsening economic climate began to take its toll and in an effort to combat declining sales Fergus turned his attention to the European market. Again he was singularly successful but it was while on his way home from a visit to a major German client four and half years ago that he was killed in a flying accident. His death left a vacuum at the apex of the company and for the following twelve months there was what might be described as a 'boardroom battle' while his sons fought for control of the company. Eventually it was the oldest son, Donald, who was elected as Chairman and Managing Director - with the voting support of his mother. But his younger brothers never accepted the situation gracefully and from time to time the personal rivalries are renewed.

All the senior executives are appointees of Donald Marsden. The senior hierarchy is shown in Figure 23.1.

FIGURE 23.1

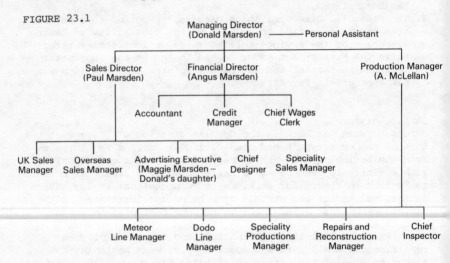

YOUR ASSIGNMENT

Study this situation critically. What do you see as the problems facing the company under the headings of:

(a) production and marketing,
(b) finance and control
(c) personnel.

What actions would you propose?

TABLE 23.2   Share of home market

(a) Mini-racers

	Marsden Meteor	Bugatti Contessa (Italy)	Aver & Thiel Prinz (Germany)	Frankel Ace (US)	Others
	(%)	(%)	(%)	(%)	(%)
last year	24.0	48.5	20.5	5.3	1.7
Year 3	27.3	42.9	22.6	7.2	-
Year 2	29.1	35.2	25.4	9.5	0.8
Year 1	30.9	30.7	28.8	9.6	-

(b) Dodgems

	Marsden	Aver & Thiel	Frankel	Others
	(%)	(%)	(%)	(%)
last year	23	49	21	7
Year 3	25	45	22	8
Year 2	26	40	24	10
Year 1	29	35	26	10

Distinguishing features of competing models

Bugatti *Contessa*: petrol driven - 275 cc - max. speed/range 65 miles, 37 kph - bodywork sheet steel panels on ashwood frame - plastic windscreen - length 290 cms - width 82 cms - weight 315 kg - cost of fuel per mile (1982 prices) 12p - list price 2.5 million lire.

Aver & Thiel *Prinz*: petrol driven - 300 cc - max speed/range 50 miles, 33 kph - bodywork sectionalised sheet steel panels - laminated windscreen - length 300 cms - width 85 cms - weight 360 kg - cost of fuel per mile (1982 prices) 15p - list price 4800 DM.

Marsden *Meteor*: battery powered - max speed/range 25 miles, 40 kph - bodywork fibre-glass on steel chassis - laminated windscreen - length 285 cms - width 80 cms - weight 250 kg - cost of fuel per mile (1982 prices) 9p - list price £1372.

Frankel *Ace*: petrol driven - 500 cc - max speed/range 75 miles, 50 kph - weight 500 kg - cost of fuel per mile (1982 prices) 25p - design similar to *Prinz* - list price $2600.

TABLE 23.3 Balance sheet as at 31 December 198- (previous year in brackets)

	(£)	(£)		(£)	(£)
Share capital (authorised and issued) ordinary stock £1 units	875,000	(875,000)	Land and buildings (at 1970 valuation)	700,000	(700,000)
General reserves	630,000	(600,000)	Plant and machinery (less depreciation)	597,372	(593,465)
Profit and loss account	1,987	(16,439)	Transporters (less depreciation)	86,200	(90,300)
Shareholders' stake	1,506,987	(1,491,439)	*Fixed assets*	1,383,572	(1,383,765)
Bank loan	525,000	(530,000)	Stocks in hand	109,465	(102,379)
Creditors	120,748	(99,418)	Work in progress	53,487	(69,818)
Provisions for tax	63,319	(58,472)	Debtors	711,556	(663,353)
Ordinary dividend	43,750	(43,750)	Cash and bank balances	1,724	(3,764)
Current liabilities	752,817	(731,640)		876,232	(839,314)
	2,259,804	(2,223,079)		2,259,804	(2,223,079)

	Year 1	Year 2	Year 3	Year 4
	(£)	(£)	(£)	(£)
Trading profit	211,546	248,515	296,563	3O1,118
Wages and salaries	1.42m	1.53m	1.70m	1.95m
Advertising	-	-	13,275	17,450

TABLE 23.4   Analysis of workforce (over past four years)

	Year 1	Year 2	Year 3	Last year
Men				
Meteor Production Line	170	172	163	160
Dodo Production Line	110	112	110	112
Miscellaneous Productions	54	52	58	63
Repairs/Reconstruction	63	71	77	82
Sales/Administration	51	52	51	54
*Women**				
Meteor Production Line	95	92	86	71
Dodo Production Line	110	105	92	82
Miscellaneous Production	31	26	20	13
Sales/Administration	47	50	54	58

* For past two years a two-shift system has been operating and
80% of the women employed have been part-timers (2 part-timers
are counted as 1 full-time worker).

TABLE 23.5   Days lost through absenteeism (in hours - 8-hour
days)

		Year 1	Year 2	Year 3	Last year
Men	certified	48445	50922	49633	49627
	uncertified	32009	33674	34672	34985
Women	certified	14987	15632	10012	8326
	uncertified	9863	8584	6250	4795

TABLE 23.6   Labour turnover (excluding redundancies)

	Year 1	Year 2	Year 3	Last year
Men				
Meteor Production Line	51	44	31	28
Dodo Production Line	17	25	2	12
Miscellaneous	15	16	18	22
Repairs/Reconstruction	10	9	10	8
Sales/Administration	6	5	5	8
Women				
Meteor Production Line	9	5	69	27
Dodo Production Line	39	39	48	23
Miscellaneous Production	25	24	25	28
Sales/Administration	19	18	20	17

TABLE 23.7   Distribution of ordinary stock of Marsden Motors Ltd (each £1 unit carries one vote)

Shareholder	No. of shares
Donald Marsden (Chairman/Managing Director)	75,000
Angus Marsden	40,000
Paul Marsden	35,000
Mrs Kate Marsden	150,000
Trustees of the estate of the late Fergus Marsden (held by Barclays Bank Trust Co. Ltd in trust for his daughter, Janet Marsden, for life and thereafter to her children)	150,000
Hibernian Engineering Co. Ltd (principal shareholder and Chairman, David Goff)	350,000
David Goff	50,000
Miscellaneous holders (average 1250 shares)	25,000

24. Hirschel Industries

Hirschel Industries Plc is the holding company in a group which
operates in the furniture industry. The company's shares are
quoted on the London Stock Exchange (on the supplementary list)
and according to the prices quoted, the equity of the company is
valued at £9.4 million. The Hirschel family - the founders of
the business - retain 18% of the voting shares and this has been
sufficient to enable them to retain control. The Hirschels
and/or their nominees are able to dominate the various boards of
directors within the group. The business was started by Abraham
Hirschel when he and his family fled from the political
disturbances in Easter Europe in 1919. Using his considerable
knowledge of and liking for timber he set up a timber import
business in the Shoreditch area of London and served the local
furniture trade. The fortunes of the business fluctuated greatly
with the general trade cycles but there was a modest expansion
over the years until Abe's oldest grandson, Mark, took over as
Chairman and Managing Director. Much of the success of the
Hirschel enterprise has been due to Mark's astuteness in taking
over certain companies at opportune moments.

The first of these was Renfrew Products Ltd, acquired in
1970. The company produces a wide range of furniture using wood
and various wood simulations. The company was experiencing cash
flow problems and was in dire need of funds. But Mark Hirschel
spotted that the problem was essentially one of over-trading.
In the boom conditions of that time the company was expanding
so quickly that debts for raw materials were accumulating at
a faster rate than the accounts were being paid by Renfrew's
customers. As one of Renfrew's creditors Mark became aware of
their predicament and bought the equity from the shareholders at
what has turned out to be a bargain price. Mark appointed his
own chief executive for Renfrew, Richard Chesney, one of the
group's most able accountants. The Renfrew operations were
integrated with those of Hirschel Industries and steps were taken
to limit the credit available to Renfrew's customers. As a result
the cash flow problem was solved and Renfrew Products not only
survived but was able to continue its expansion - if at a reduced
rate in a more difficult economic climate.

Another company to become a wholly owned subsidiary of
Hirschel's was Halliday's National Furniture Stores Ltd. This
company operates a total of seventeen super furniture stores
on the outskirts of all the major towns in England and Wales.
Trevor Halliday had died in 1973 and his company had been valued
on a break-up basis to assess his estate's liability for death duty

(or capital transfer tax as it is now). Trevor's widow and
daughter had been obliged to raise funds from the sale of
the company's shares. There had been a boom in property but
values were now beginning to tumble. Mark Hirschel had heard of
their predicament and did a rescue act by offering them shares
in Hirschel Industries in exchange for the Halliday's equity.
The offer was accepted with alacrity and Hirschel Industries was
able to integrate the business with their own emerging group.

The third subsidiary in the Hirschel group is Harper Page
Transport Services Ltd. This company established itself as a
national carrier service but specialised in the furniture removal
business, carrying the contents of homes when people switch
houses..They also offer a depository service in two large
warehouses on the outskirts of Reading and Leicester. The
business was badly affected by a slump in the housing market in
1980-1 and when the company's bankers called in their £100,000
loan it seemed as if Harper Page Transport Services would be
wound up. Once again Mark Hirschel performed a rescue act by
offering shares in Hirschel in exchange for the Harper Page
equity. This time the Chairman and Managing Director of the
company, Gregory Page, was also allowed to remain as chief
executive and was offered a seat on the board of Hirschels.
The Harper Page fleet of lorries became fully utilised within
the group and the depositories at Reading and Leicester
became the key distribution centres for the group.

The vertical amalgamation of the companies in the group has
achieved considerable economies of scale which has given the
group a competitive edge in the various markets they serve.
Group profits have risen steadily and further expansion is
planned. Yet in spite of the successes, problems of co-ordinating
effort within the group are beginning to appear.

One of Mark Hirschel's present objectives is to replace the
fleet of Harper Page lorries and vans, many of which are out of
date and expensive in terms of maintenance and fuel. The cost of
this exercise is likely to exceed £500,000 and in order to fund
this operation Mark is using the profits generated by Renfrew
Products. This is creating problems for Renfrew's chief executive.
A number of new products have been manufactured and launched on the
market but have failed to reach their expected level of sales and
had to be withdrawn. This has added to the drain on profits at
Renfrew and Richard Chesney has visited Mark Hirschel on a number
of occasions complaining that the funds being transferred from
Renfrew to Harper Page (in the form of interest-free intra-group
loans) are seriously inhibiting Renfrew's operations.

The group's chief executive was unrepentant.

'It's my decision how group profits are used', he said.
'Renfrew Products are just part of the group. And in any case
you would have more funds available if you were more successful
in your product launches.'

'I accept your responsibility for the group's performance.
Obviously you've got to take an overview. And I accept that we've
made some mistakes in our marketing of new designs. But we've
learned from our mistakes. We've learned that we need more money
spent on market research - getting the feel of the market we're
aiming at - and we need a more effective advertising campaign.

We've learned that it's not just a question of spending on advertising: timing is just as important. The trouble is we're not getting the opportunity to put our experience to good use. If we aren't able to develop and market new products you won't have to worry about how our profits are utilised. We shan't be making any.'

The forceful approach proved effective. After studying some of the figures provided by Chesney, Mark Hirschel relented. It was agreed that the group would obtain the funds they required for modernising Harper and Page's transport fleet from a rights issue to the Hirschel ordinary shareholders. In the meantime a directive would be issued to the chief executive of each of the subsidiaries informing them that, with immediate effect, each company in the group will be allowed to retain their own profits for expansion and that they must not rely on the support of the group for financial assistance. Intra-group loans will be possible but at negotiated rates of interest, with the group chief executive as arbiter if required. Within a few days of this directive circulating Chesney had visited Gregory Page and they had agreed the £100,000 loan from Renfrew to Harper Page would henceforth carry interest at a rate of 8% per annum.

Comforted by the outcome of his efforts Chesney was shattered a week later when he was shown the new tariff which had been sent to all Harper Page customers. The transport charges were going up by an average of 12½%. Although Renfrew Products benefit from a special 15% 'favoured customer' discount, the new charges were a blow to them. Chesney referred to his latest half-yearly accounts. Transport charges amounted to £27,500. He was very angry.

That happened three months ago. This morning Mark Hirschel received a telephone call from Gregory Page.

'Sorry to bother you this early in the morning, Mr Hirschel,' he said, 'but I've got a crisis on my hands. I've just got the latest revenue account and we're down by nearly a third. My first reaction was to think it was either a genuine decline in the trade or the result of our recent increase in charges. But then I looked at our account with Renfrew. It's there where we've lost the volume of trade. I've made some discreet enquiries and I've discovered that Richard Chesney is using other carriers. If he keeps on like this we'll be out of business within twelve months.'

Mark Hirschel got through to Chesney at Renfrew Products. He told him what he had just heard.

'Yes,' said Chesney, 'it's quite true. Adelphi are able to offer us a superior service at a much lower price - even allowing for the 15% discount.'

YOUR ASSIGNMENT
1. What action would you advise Mark Hirschel to take in these circumstances?
2. Produce a draft document such as might be used to clarify the group's policy on intra-group operations.
3. Hirschel Industries are contemplating making a rights issue in order to raise £350,000 to modernise the carrier fleet of

Harper Page Transport Services. Produce an outline plan
showing the terms on which the rights might be issued to
the shareholders (e.g., 1 for 4 at a price of 20p per share).
The capital structure of the holding company is as follows:

ordinary stock units of 25p each	£5,000,000
8% non-cumulative preference stock	
units of £1 each	£1,000,000
general reserves	£3,752,000

The middle price of the Hirschel Industry ordinary stock is
47p at the present time. The price has varied between 39p and
58p over the past twelve months.

4. What are the merits and demerits of this method of raising
   funds from the point of view of (a) the company and (b) the
   shareholders?

Guidelines

There is no intention here to provide finite solutions to the
problems raised in the case studies. Rather the intention is to
indicate some of the ideas which might emerge. More help is
provided in relation to the earlier cases and the input is
reduced in the later stages as students are assumed to have
become familiar with the appropriate decision-making techniques.
At all times the notes which follow should be viewed as
stimulating and not restrictive.

1. TALISMAN TECHNICS

FIGURE G.1   Graph showing the costs/revenue at different levels
of output/sales

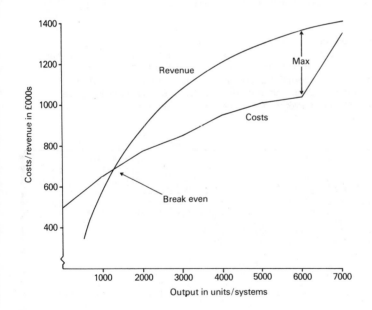

Break-even   At an output of around 1250 units revenue would
begin to exceed costs – assuming all units are sold. In other
words at this point the business begins to make a profit.
    Maximisation of profits is achieved at an output of 6000 units

at which point the gap between revenue and costs is greatest.

*Brief job description for sales representatives Job function/
duties:*
(1) Visit clients responding to various forms of advertisement.
(2) Write letters to clients and communicate with them by
    telephone.
(3) Set up models for demonstration in homes and offices.
(4) Answer questions of a technical nature regarding the products.
(5) Sell security equipment - initially to householders, later
    to firms.
(6) Complete financial arrangements for payment of accounts.
(7) Instil confidence in clients and act with integrity at all
    times.
(8) Revisit clients after installation of system to ensure client
    is satisfied with system.
(9) Compile routine sales reports.
(10)Available to meet clients at any time - including weekends.

Advertisement for staff
Present advertisement might attract unscrupulous characters. In
this job a high level of motivation needs to be coupled with a
high level of integrity. Retired servicemen and police officers
would make ideal recruits. The wording might be amended to
emphasise the need for proved integrity.

Major problem confronting the company
The report which follows indicates the general nature of the
problems which are likely to be encountered. The form of the
report may vary according to individual taste, but there is
merit in using sub-headings as this makes the report more
readable. It also makes it easy for the reader to refer back to
specific points.

To Mr S Schornberg   From Mr A N Other
                                            Personal Assistant
                                            (date)
Problems anticipated for Talisman Technics Ltd

As requested, this report is aimed at drawing attention to the
areas in which problems might be expected to arise in the
short and medium terms. In many ways the problems envisaged
here are the typical problems faced by a comparatively small
concern which is enjoying a rapid growth.

Organisation and communication
As the business expands it will be necessary to set up a
formal organisation structure - delegating various specialist
functions to selected staff. For example, bearing in mind the
special qualities called for in the sales force, it may prove
advisable to appoint a personnel manager before very long.
The role of a personnel manager would be both to select
appropriate staff and plan for staffing generally as operations
expand and more staff become involved. By the same token a sales
manager could be employed to ensure that the sales force are
functioning effectively and be made responsible for carrying out
the selling policy as laid down by the directors. When powers

are delegated in this fashion it is essential to define the
responsibilities unambiguously, so that the staff in question
know precisely what is expected from them. The merit of delegating is that the directors will have some of the burdens of
routine administration removed from their shoulders and will
be able to concentrate on the decisions related to major
policies and strategies.

As growth proceeds and departmentalisation of the business
develops communication problems are inevitable. Whereas at
present the directors are personally aware of all that is
happening, in an enlarged organisation their information will
be 'second hand' or passed on by others. In this system an
adequate feedback becomes essential as a means of exercising
control and co-ordination. Targets will need to be set. Rules
and regulations will need to be framed so as to set out the
parameters of behaviour for the members of the organisation.
The problem then becomes to ensure that motivation for employees
remains high in spite of the constraints imposed.

Marketing and competition

The Talisman products are obviously attractive and highly
marketable and this is bound to put them under the scrutiny
of would-be competitors. Patenting the sensory device is the
obvious defence. However, it is to be expected that similar
devices will be developed — perhaps by larger organisations
with sophisticated marketing departments. On the one hand
Talisman Technics can do with as much publicity as possible
locally. On the other hand, a low profile in the initial stages
would give the company an opportunity to progress before major
competitors become aware of the operations which are taking
place.

There is no great merit in stimulating demand through
advertising and publicity unless there is a productive capacity to
match the demand. Unsatisfied demand is merely making it easier
for competitors to fill the breach. The basic problem is that
we have here a product which undoubtedly has a national market,
but the backing organisation is not large enough to take
advantage of the situation. The danger is that by the time
Talisman move on from South Yorkshire they might find the
remaining markets taken over by competitors.

One way of limiting competition would be to keep prices low,
but this would tend to erode the advantage of being first in
the market with a new product.

Finance and cash flow

There is already a deficiency of working capital. Current assets
should exceed current liabilities substantially in order to
ensure the company's solvency. In Talisman's balance sheet the
creditors exceed the current assets by £10,757.75 – £5,457.75 =
£5,300.00. There is no danger of immediate insolvency since the
bank has offered overdraft facilities, but the company is very
much at the mercy of the bank. The bank loan will presumably be
for a fixed term. By what date is the loan due to be repaid?
What would happen if the loan were not repaid by then? In order
to avoid a financial crisis such as this it is vitally important
to plough back profits to the required extent.

If the shortage of liquid funds is of a temporary nature, the
provision of a short-term overdraft is an appropriate remedy.
If, however, the capital deficiency is more permanent then further
ordinary shares or debentures should be issued — always assuming
the necessary funds can be found. One of the dangers with the
cash flow in a rapidly expanding business is that debts will be
incurred long before clients pay for the installation of their
system. The problem, described as over-trading, is compounded
if credit terms are offered to purchasers and can lead to a
cash flow deficiency even though the business is flourishing
according to sales figures and (paper) profits.

Conclusion

There would be obvious advantages if the Talisman operation could
come under the umbrella of a larger organisation which would
presumably be able to provide (a) staff expertise in the fields
of personnel, marketing and finances, etc., and (b) finance — by
acquiring shares and/or debentures (perhaps convertible debentures)
This would enable the expansion of Talisman to proceed without

2: THE DOWNHILL RUN

Which of the two existing models should be jettisoned to make way
for the new *Challenger*?

To calculate moving averages - say twelve-monthly moving
averages - add sales for a particular model for twelve months
(January to December inclusive) and divide this total by 12 to
find the average monthly sales. In the graph shown in Figure G.2
this is plotted at the mid-point of the year, between the months
of June and July. Next, add sales for the twelve months from
February to January inclusive - again divide this total by 12
and calculate the average monthly sales. The average is plotted
at the point between July and August. The resultant plots will
enable a trend line to be drawn and a projection to be made -
forecasting future sales. An alternative treatment would be to
use quarterly (three-monthly) moving averages - calculated on the
same principle - aggregating three months' sales then averaging
them and centring the plot on the middle month. The demerit in
this is that it would not show such a flattened trend line and
so forecasting would be more difficult.

FIGURE G.2   Graph showing 12-monthly moving averages and
projected trends for existing Downhill models

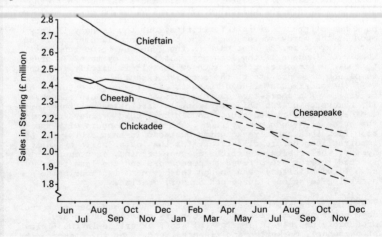

146

Sales of the *Chieftain* are obviously falling at a faster rate than other models and it will soon be earning less than the other models. The trends for the *Chickadee* are less definite but sales are below those of the *Cheetah* and *Chesapeake* and show no signs of picking up. So on this evidence and, assuming that unit costs are the same for each model, it is the *Chickadee* and the *Chieftain* which should be dropped.

One can see from these dismal forecasts why a new and up-dated model is so necessary and why the redundancies are developing.

Redundancy problem

Total workforce = 4,186
Redundancies required in three months = 628 (15% of 4186)
Further redundancies required in nine months = 419 (10% of 4186)

Options include:

1. Ask for volunteers for early retirement, bearing in mind some workers would stand to receive substantial redundancy pay. Long servers would stand to gain most.
2. Employ the principle of last in, first out, but this would tend to penalise the younger workers since out of 1170 workers with less than two years' service, 753 (75%) are under 21.
3. Allow natural wastage to take its toll. According to the bar charts shown in Figure 2.2, 3520 workers left in the last three years, i.e. 1173 per annum.

$$\text{Labour turnover} = \frac{1173}{4186} \times 100 = 28\%$$

So, in three months 293 workers will leave the firm (7% of 4186) and in nine months 586 more workers will leave (14% of 4186) - see Table G.1. There would also presumably be some older workers retiring - these are not included in Table G.1. In these circumstances the union might argue that if all recruitment was stopped for, say, one year there would be no need to make any of the existing workers redundant. But of course it does not follow, from management's point of view, that workers who leave are going to be the ones they want to lose. A transferring and retraining programme would need to be initiated by the company.

TABLE G.1   Natural wastage compared to redundancy requirements

Time	Nos to be made redundant	Nos lost through natural wastage	Shortfall/ Surplus
In 3 mths	628	293	-335
In 9 mths	419	586	+167
Totals	1047	879	-168

3. 'A TIGER IN YOUR TANK'

A. *Workers' shares*
Merits
(1) Gives workers a stake in the prosperity of the company.
(2) Should change attitudes to waste and inefficiency.
(3) Should reduce the propensity for taking industrial action – strikes, go-slows, etc.
(4) Should discourage absenteeism and labour turnover.

Demerits
(1) If share prices fall the scheme will be invalid as a motivator and will be counter-productive in having raised workers' expectations.
(2) Some workers will not be able to understand/appreciate how they stand to benefit.
(3) Some workers will sell shares as soon as they acquire them.
(4) The scheme involves administrative expense.

B. *Works council*
Merits
(1) Grievances can be aired to senior managers.
(2) Management's views, plans and problems can be made known to the workforce, with the benefit of an immediate feedback.
(3) The experience could be cathartic for workers.
(4) Workforces might be more prepared to accept change if they have participated in the decision-making process.

Demerits
(1) Discussion is time-consuming – and costly to that extent.
(2) Only a small proportion of workers are involved: the remainder may remain uninformed and unmotivated.
(3) Workers will have little to contribute in some areas.
(4) Insensitive control of the proceedings might crystallise divisions rather than remove them.

C. *Good-timekeeping bonus*
Merits
(1) Reduced absenteeism and lateness.
(2) Effects are immediate and measurable.
(3) May be introduced within the normal bargaining process for wage increases – in which case the financial burden is less than it seems.
(4) Rewards workers who obey the rules – encourages compliance.

Demerits
(1) There is a danger in equating attendance with performance.
(2) Innocent parties will sometimes suffer – as when buses are late or there is a genuine health problem or domestic crisis.
(3) Once a worker has lost the bonus the device may be counter-productive.
(4) This ploy is an admission that normal supervisory skills are inadequate.

D. Removal of management-worker barriers

Merits
(1) Avoidance of duplicated catering arrangements.
(2) Removal of petty irritations as far as workers are concerned.
(3) Names on overalls would be ego-satisfying and make work less impersonal.
(4) Two-way communication improved with informal idea exchange (in canteen).

Demerits
(1) Loss of privacy inhibiting managers' discussions.
(2) Will be seen as a levelling down by some managers/supervisors.
(3) A few workers may monopolise managers in the canteen.
(4) Workers may see managers as 'spies' in the canteen.

E. Job enrichment

Merits
(1) Should reduce labour turnover, absenteeism and lateness.
(2) Encourages personal development - greater job satisfaction.
(3) Adverse effects of boredom should be minimised.
(4) If workers are consulted it will be an indication that management is making an effort to improve the workers' lot.

Demerits
(1) Some workers may see it as an attempt to get more work for the same pay.
(2) It may prove increasingly difficult to enrich jobs - the law of diminishing returns will apply to successive applications.
(3) Unions may resist - possibility of demarcation problems.
(4) The technique needs to be applied by experts.

Control over subsidiaries/subordinates
(1) Set targets (after discussion) but allow subsidiaries/ subordinates to achieve the targets in their own way.
(2) Periodically check performance in relation to target: discuss deviations and corrective action to be taken.

4. M. S. MARDI GRAS
If the voyage time-share option were exercised the proceeds would be as shown in Table G.2. The gross proceeds would be £11.598 million less unspecified costs for advertising, legal disbursements and administrative expenses. This has to be compared to the £9.5 million offered for the Mardi Gras by the rival shipping line.
    Either of these options is preferable to continuing the operations of the past five years which have produced substantial losses in two of the last three years.

149

TABLE G.2

Deck		Number of cabins (a)	Total receipts per deck for 52 weeks £000s (b)	Total receipts from sales £s million (a) x (b)
Main		14	110	1.540
Upper:	inner	34	76	2.584
	outer	34	89	3.026
Boat:	inner	32	63	2.016
	outer	32	76	2.432
				11.598

Voyage time share
Merits
(1) Provided expenses do not exceed £2,098,000 this is the best
    of the options.
(2) At the end of thirty years - assuming there is 'scrap value' -
    the Mardi Gras would become fully available to the owners
    again.
(3) Moderate profits could still be earned through the operations
    of the management company.
(4) The management company which would be running the ship would
    be under the control of the owners.

Pitfalls
(1) The calculations showing £11.5 million proceeds assumes a
    100% take-up, but anything less than an 83% take-up

    allowing £98,000 for expenses $\left\{ \frac{9.5}{11.5} \times 100 = 83\% \right\}$ and a

    straightforward sale would be preferable.
(2) Disputes are bound to arise if and when voyages are cancelled,
    especially if some time shares suffer more than others. Legal
    expenses - perhaps compensation - will become payable.
(3) Purchasers may find the cruises on offer unattractive, a lot
    of time would be spent on the ocean as the present voyages are
    planned. Many cruises now include a flight out to the port
    of departure so that more time can be spent in exotic ports,
    etc.
(4) As the ship gets older the repairs and maintenance charges
    will increase; insurance cover likewise.

FIGURE G.3   One possible organisation structure for the M. S.
Mardi Gras

5.   AVA ADVERTISING AGENCY – IN-TRAY
A few thoughts on three of the problems to be dealt with:

The accounts
No depreciation charged on fixed assets yet? No provision for
bad debts or taxation? Drawings could be seen as possible only
because of the bank loan? Two items not shown (though they
could conceivably be included in Other Expenses) – interest on
bank loan and insurance. Nearly one half of the commissions, etc.
(£333,560) have not yet been collected from the clients
(commissions unpaid are £137,652 – see Sundry debtors).
Explanation for large sum spent on advertising required. Is it
AVA's own advertising or sums spent on behalf of clients? If the
latter, different treatment in the accounts called for?

Speech to Rotary Club on advertising
Advertising often seen as a waste of resources. It creates demand
rather than satisfies. It pushes up prices. It is used to
restrict the entry of competitors. *But* it is a boon to the
businessman (and perhaps to society) because when sales begin
to fall:

(1) The businessman is faced with the need to reduce output which
    leads to a reduction in the workforce. Instead he stimulates
    sales by advertising and retains his workforce intact.
(2) The business will be tempted to reduce prices. This would be
    pleasing to the consumer, but prices will be compensatingly
    high when sales pick up again. Instead, by advertising, sales
    are stimulated and prices can be stabilised. Of course prices
    will rise with inflation, but this is divorced from the
    present argument.
(3) The stocks of the businessman will accumulate – yet to hold
    stocks is expensive – and the cost will be passed on to the
    consumer. Instead the businessman advertises and in doing so
    helps to minimise his stockholdings. Note the interrelation-
    ship between stocks and sales.

An open plan office
Merits
(1) Less restrictions in movement and workflow.
(2) Easier supervision: staff are easier to see - and control.
(3) More flexibility in arranging workflows - no barriers.

Demerits
(1) More distractions - unless screens are used.
(2) More noise - unless sound absorption techniques are used.
(3) Lack of privacy - especially for interviewing clients in this sort of work - but also creates difficulties for staff discussions of a confidential nature.

Staff consultation
Merits
(1) Subordinates might have useful contributions to make: either by extending the range of options considered, or in evaluating them.
(2) They will be motivated by involvement (ego food/catharsis) and more readily accept change.
(3) Provides a useful feedback for manager; an opportunity to clarify instructions and gauge reactions.

Demerits
(1) Discussion takes time and many decisions require immediate response.
(2) Subordinates may be frustrated if their contributions are either rejected or ignored.
(3) In some areas of work the subordinates will have little to contribute.

6. THE ELECTRONIC KNITTING MACHINE
Questions likely to be asked by bank manager
1. How much is required and why is it required?
2. When is repayment intended and how will the funds for repayment be generated?
3. What risks are associated with the project?
4. What securities/collaterals are available?
5. What evidence is there that a market exists for the new machines?
6. What sort of production difficulties are likely to be encountered?

Threats related to the project
1. Competitors might be able to improve on the new machine, especially when it is exported.
2. A competitor might have more funds available for advertising - or might have access to a superior distribution network.
3. Potential clients might associate the new venture with the failure of George Ascham and Sons Ltd. They may be reluctant to do business or grant credit.
4. After-sales service might be expected by purchasers of a product such as this.
5. No sign that Justin Ascham is contemplating forming a limited

152

company at this stage. A company would be the essential form
for this operation. He stands to lose all his personal
possessions and his inheritance if the business fails.
6. The bank may turn down his application for a loan - or offer
him an insufficient sum. This could mean he is unable to take
advantage of the situation.

Opportunities related to the project
1. Possibilities exist for exporting to a number of countries
according to the marketing consultants' report. Perhaps it
would be wise to concentrate on a limited area initially. The
South American group is attractive because of the lack of
competition but it is a distant market and little information
is available. The most attractive market listed is probably
Group Two - Scandinavia. The market is fairly compact and
competing machines are outdated. There is the language
problem of course and the German competitors are ominously
close to the market. (What are the present exchange rates
for these countries?)
2. There is £100,000 tied up in his late father's estate - half
of which is due to Justin as a remainderman though this will
be subject to Capital Transfer Tax on his mother's death.
These funds would be invaluable to the business - particularly
if the bank refuses the loan facilities. If a company is to
be floated his family/the estate could buy shares or
debentures. The mother and two sons, only beneficiaries in the
estate, could break the trust. Who should Justin approach
first? His mother? The trustees? Or his brother? What
inducements could he offer?

FIGURE G.4   Break-even chart

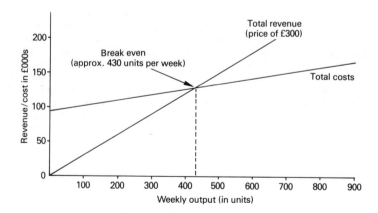

7. DATELINE LAGOS
James Adesina's report would include reference to:

Nkamanu personality test
When testing procedures are applied for job candidates one
would expect to find a correlation between success in the test
and success in the work situation. The scatter diagram, however,
shows that some who did well in the test turned out to be poor
salesmen. In fact the test seems to have little predictive value.

Wokoma selection test
By contrast this test was able to identify those likely to be
the best salesmen. Those who scored high marks in the test
(the crosses represent individuals) also achieved high sales in
the field. This test has predictive value and should therefore
be retained.

Moving averages
Twelve monthly? There is an opportunity here to produce a
sales forecast for the company as a whole and also to compare
growth in each of the three branches. (See Chapter 2 - The
Downhill Run - for a worked example of trends calculated from
moving averages.)

Job enrichment for motivating salesmen
According to Professor F. Herzberg's hygiene-motivation theory
the salesmen might be expected to respond favourably by being
allowed more discretions. The situation in this Nigerian company
is similar to that at ICI Dulux Paints Division when the job
enrichment technique was first applied in Britain. The results
of those experiments are fully set out in the *Harvard Business
Review* (March-April 1969) in an article by William J. Paul, Keith
B. Robertson and Frederick Herzberg. On this evidence Francis
Wokoma's proposals seem reasonable.

Decentralisation (regarding recent crisis over reprographics)
As the business expands the weight of the decisions made at
headquarters is bound to increase. If the central authority is
over-burdened major policy decisions could be adversely affected
through the congestion of work. The whole organisation could
suffer.
    As a business expands there is bound to be a lengthening of the
chain of command - in Ebokpomwen's business even the physical
distance between branches is great. Headquarters is better suited
to make decisions in that it has an overall picture of the
business, but it has to act on reports prepared at lower levels
and these are bound to be distorted to some extent. Certain
advantages would be gained by giving more discretion to the branch
managers, *inter alia*:

(1) Local managers are 'at the scene of action': their decisions
    can be speedier and related to the local situation.
(2) The delegation of more responsibility to them should produce
    a positive and favourable response - see 'job enrichment'
    above.

(3) When top managers are relieved of the burden of routine decision-making they can give more time to planning. There will be fewer crises if problems can be anticipated.

(4) Delegation of decision-making powers could improve efficiency within the organisation so long as standards of performance are laid down (as when a full budgetary system is introduced) together with an adequate programme of appraisal and the necessary checks to eradicate any deviations from these standards.

8. HORDER AND ZIFF PHARMACEUTICS

On the subject of decentralisation see guidelines for previous case. Which of the Delta Nine injection variants is most effective in delaying the advance of cancer? The scatter diagram in Figure G.5 suggests Variant 1 is most efficacious.

FIGURE G.5

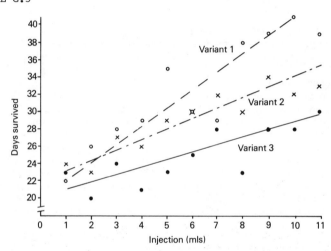

What can be gleaned from the research on the Q-virus? The statistical evidence indicates that the vaccination procedure is more effective than treating the Q-virus after diagnosis?

Animal experiments/vivisection, etc.
Merits
(1) Short gestation period.
(2) Genetic effects can be studied.
(3) Inexpensive.
(4) Animals such as rats do not rouse sympathy.
(5) Better to make mistakes on animals than humans.

Limitations
(1) Animals though intelligent do not have complex human

psychologies.
(2) Contempt for animals leads to contempt for human life.
(3) Who decides what experiments are necessary?
(4) Subsequent tests on humans still required.
(5) Gives great offence to some people.

Staff resistance to change

Why should there be resistance? Staff may fear greater domination
by US executives - loss of status - even loss of jobs. They
would need to adjust to new relationships, new lines of
communication, new chains of command. Rumours would fill any
communication vacuums. How could they be persuaded to accept the
changes?

Explain the proposals fully to London staff and listen to
them. Answer their questions. Allow them to participate in the
decision-making process. Reassure staff who feel threatened -
guarantee jobs/pay, etc.

9. THE OFFICE MANAGER - IN-TRAY

Some thoughts on the responses to the in-tray items:

Letter from Jays

If the company is unable to pay its debts then it should be
wound up by the court? How much is owed to us? Should we present
a petition to the High Court? Section 346 of the Companies Act
1948 provides that the court, in all matters relating to the
winding up of a company, shall have 'regard to the wishes of the
creditors'. In *Re J. D. Swain Ltd* (1965) it was held that where
the majority of the creditors were of the opinion that there
should be no winding up at all, the petitioning creditor would
still be entitled to a winding up. In short, we have rights in
these matters and should ensure that our interests are protected.

Note from Paula

Job grading involves dividing up the job hierarchy into a number
of pay groups or grades, developing written definitions for
each grade, and then assigning every job to a particular grade.
In the words of Dale S. Beach:

'In order to construct a grade description scale, the basic
information must come from descriptions of all the jobs
involved. As in much job evaluation work it is best to use a
committee to take advantage of pooled judgment in arriving at
decisions. The committee must actually set up a rank-order
list of a large representative sample of all the jobs in the
organisation, giving consideration to duties, skills,
abilities, responsibilities, and other differentiating
qualities. These jobs are then grouped into classes or grades
that represent different pay levels ranging from low to
high . . .'
(*Personnel: the Management of People at Work*, 2nd edn, Collier-
Macmillan, 1970)

Note from Jamah Singh
Figure G.6 shows a frequency distribution for the combined ranges
of shoes. Similar charts could be produced for each of the High
Fashion and Standard ranges. Comparisons could be helpful.

FIGURE G.6

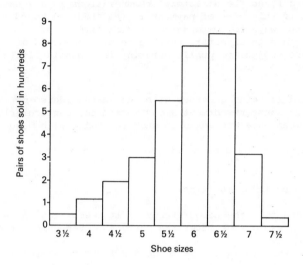

One of the problems for the Production Department would be
to know how many shoes of each size to produce. Hence the value
of statistical records:

Measures of dispersion? For High Fashion range:

Standard deviation = 0.8
Lower quartile = 5.5 (5½)
Upper quartile = 6.5 (6½)
Median = 6.0
Arithmetic mean = 6.0

Or percentages in present ranges could be projected. For example,
in the High Fashion range 25.8 per cent are size 6, 29.2 per cent
are size 6½.

10.   THE BOARD MEETING – GROUP ROLE PLAY
Largely a matter of group interaction, but regarding items 1 and
2 on the Agenda a calculation is required to discover the effects
of any proposals on the holding company's profit (with the
Chairman's interest particularly in mind).

Golden handshakes
Pros
(1) An encouragement to the other directors as well – they are

presumably expected to make considerable efforts on the company's behalf.
(2) Encourages confidentiality even when a director has left the company – much of the boardroom discussion/information is likely to be of a private and confidential nature.
(3) If such payments have become conventional a director may well feel aggrieved.
(4) The board fixes the directors' remunerations in any case, so that if this sort of payment is resisted the board will find other ways to compensate retiring directors.
(5) All payments to directors have to be disclosed and are therefore subject to public scrutiny in a public limited company.

Cons
(1) The board is being generous with the shareholders' money.
(2) Likely to cause resentment among workforce, particularly if and when they are asked to show restraint with wage claims.
(3) Such payments could be considered as unproductive.

Donations to political parties
Pros
(1) The unions fund the Labour Party so it seems reasonable for big business to look after the party that recognises their importance.
(2) Payments such as this have to be disclosed to shareholders and they can raise their objections if they so wish.
(3) There is presumably a possibility that the company which makes substantial payments to a political party will be able to exert some pressure to ensure that policies favourable to the company are pursued.

Cons
(1) All payments to political parties (by groups?) are unethical?
(2) Management v. worker conflicts are exacerbated.

Group Personnel Director's Report
Among controversial topics will no doubt be the proposal to use more women in the workforce. Is this an example of sex discrimination? Which sex is being favoured? Is such a policy justifiable? How can equal opportunity legislation be enforced in practice? Do you think the report should have been phrased differently?

11.   THE EMBASSY COURT HOTEL
How to calculate profit for the year at the Northcliffe Hotel
What were the net assets at the start of the year? What were they at the end? The difference represents profit (or loss) for the year.
    According to the information available the latest balance sheet would read as in Table G.3.

TABLE G.3   Balance sheet of Northcliffe Hotel as at 31 December last

	(£)		(£)
Capital account	41,138	Cash at bank	7,501
Add profit for the year*+	61,026	Stock of food and drink	507
	102,164	Rates in advance	920
Less drawings for the year	2,500	Kitchen equipment and tableware 1,551	
	99,664	*Less* depreciation 551	1,000
Creditors - Wine 112		Furniture and	
Taxes 568	680	bed linen 3,496	
		Less depreciation 2,330	1,166
		Premises†	89,250
	100,344		100,344

* This will appear as a balancing figure in the Profit and Loss Account (it will include the cash receipts from clients which will be assumed to be net).
+ These profits will be subject to tax and will reduce considerably the funds available. This figure is likely to be much lower in the current year if the Lloyds students are no longer staying at the hotel.
† The question should be raised as to whether the value of the premises has increased since 1975. What would be the effect of a revaluation on the balance sheet?

Purchase of the Embassy Court
It will be cheaper to buy 60% of the 150,000 ordinary shares. This would give the Colbornes control of the hotel for 90,000 x £1.75 = £157,500.

Benefits of having two hotels would include: possibility of interchanging staff, if and when required; possibility of switching bookings when one hotel is full; and possibility of closing one hotel out of season.

12. THE PURBECK HOLIDAY CAMPUS

Claim under fire insurance policy
A contract of insurance is *uberrimae fidei,* i.e. a contract based on utmost good faith. The assured is expected to disclose any relevant fact and this would include any change in material circumstances which might adversely affect the degree of risk borne by the insurance company. However, the insurance company would not be able to avoid the contract if they had been notified of the situation and had not disclaimed liability.

The bankruptcy

On this evidence S. Smith should receive £9,000 from the London dealer $\left(\frac{15}{100} \times \pounds 60,000\right)$. This should give him the following assets in due course:

Sum due from bankrupt dealer	£ 9,000
Other assets	£ 4,000
Total assets	£13,000

$$\frac{\text{Assets}}{\text{Liabilities}} = \frac{\pounds 13,000}{\pounds 68,000} \times 100 = 19\text{p in the } \pounds \text{ to be paid to S. Smith's creditors.}$$

So, Purbeck Holiday Campus can expect (eventually)

$$\frac{19}{100} \times \pounds 35,000 = \pounds 6,650$$

In the meantime they should show the S. Smith account as a bad debt in their accounts.

Is there any substance in the query regarding the consideration for the caravans? There is an assumption in the law of contract that the parties to a contract have behaved 'commercially'. They are expected to have stood on their own feet and made their own bargains. *Caveat emptor* ('buyer beware') is the guiding maxim. In the absence of fraud or misrepresentation, the courts will not assist a party who complains he has made a bad bargain. Thus, provided that Purbeck Holiday Campus has given some consideration, it will be no defence for Smith (or his creditor) to plead that the caravans were over-priced. It is assumed there has been no breach of warranty.

13. 'THREE'S A CROWD . . .'

The law relating to partnership is set out in the Partnership Act 1890, which defines a partnership as the 'relationship which subsists between persons carrying on a business in common with a view to profit'. Every partner may take part in the management of the partnership business (Section 24 (5)) No partner shall be entitled to remuneration for acting in the partnership business (Section 24 (6)). Differences between the partners in matters connected with the ordinary business of the partnership may be settled by a majority in number of the partners, regardless of the capital introduced by each (Section 24 (7) and (8)). Every partner in a firm is liable jointly with the other partners for all the debts and obligations of the firm - without limit (section 9). All partners have implied authority to engage and dismiss employees (Section 5). Individuals who by words spoken or written or by conduct allow themselves to be represented as partners are liable as partners (Section 14 (1)). Note advisability of a formal partnership deed as a means of avoiding destructive disputes.

The dismissal

The situation is governed by the Employment Protection Act 1975, among others. Not only must it be shown that the employers had a fair reason for dismissal, it must also be shown that they went about the dismissal fairly dealing with an immediate problem in a reasonable way. In the case of inefficiency ample warnings might be considered necessary so that the assistant, Julie, might have had a chance to improve. A warning does not have to be in writing but it adds force to the employers' arguments for dismissal. If a criminal offence has been committed dismissal will be deemed fair if the employers can show that they could not reasonably be expected to employ her in the shop in the light of her particular offence. However, nothing has been proved and the employers will have to beware of making accusations which cannot be substantiated (either in writing - libellous - or orally - slanderous).

Any complaint of unfair dismissal must be presented to an Industrial Tribunal within three months of the dismissal. If the claim is upheld by the tribunal it may order (a) reinstatement (or re-engagement) or (b) compensation which does not depend simply on financial loss but is based on factors such as age, wage and length of service.

14. THE TAKEOVER

Share valuations in the two companies? On a break-up basis, assuming the balance sheet figures can be justified, valuations should match the figures in Table G.4.

TABLE G.4

G. Sorrell and Son (Stores) Ltd		J. P. Hardwick and Sons Ltd	
	(£)		(£)
Total assets	1,655,824	Assets less goodwill	6,231,000
Liabilities	569,842	Liabilities	2,398,000
Net assets	1,085,982	Net assets	3,833,000
Assets per share		Assets per stock unit	

$$£ \ \frac{1,085,982}{100,000} = £10.86 \qquad\qquad £ \ \frac{3,833,000}{8,000,000} = 48p$$

Offer for £10.86 share amounts to:

3 stock units worth 48p	=	£1.44
plus cash	=	£2.50
		£3.94

But consider the effect if a substantial part of general reserves in Sorrell and Son, say £400,000, is capitalised before the exchange takes place. Sorrell's balance sheet would then show:

Ordinary shares of £1 each	500,000
General reserves	500,000

Amended value of assets per share:

$$£\ \frac{1,085,982}{500,000} = £2.17$$

15. THE HONG KONG OPTIONS

What services are offered by the Export Credits Guarantee Department? This British government department provides a special type of insurance facility covering risks not normally dealt with by the commercial insurers. Cover is offered with regard to the creditworthiness of overseas buyers and also with reference to economic and political risks arising from events in overseas countries. Two broad categories of insurance are available:

(1) The Comprehensive Short-term guarantee, offering compensation up to 90% if the loan is the result of the buyer's insolvency or refusal to accept the goods which have been dispatched to him. The cover is increased to 95% if the losses result from war, political events, withdrawal of licences, etc. Under this sort of contract it is necessary for the exporter to arrange all or most of his export business comprehensively with the ECGD.

(2) Supplier/Buyer Credits. These are specific policies which have to be negotiated for each contract. With a Supplier Credit the manufacturer sells on credit (which may be long term) and the cover is then against specified risks. In the case of a Buyer Credit the exporter receives the cash promptly through the medium of a British bank. This amounts to a loan from the bank - repayable by instalments - the loan being guaranteed to the bank by the ECGD.

16. Z12 INSECT REPELLENT

Which of the Capital Structures being considered would be best suited to the oil company? Consider situation at seven different levels of profit shown in Table G.5:

TABLE G.5

| Level of profit prior to debenture service and dividends (£s) | Distributions in £s | | | | | |
| | Oil company | | | Chemical company | | |
	Option 1	Option 2	Option 3	Option 1	Option 2	Option 3
25,000	nil	17,857	23,000	25,000	7,143	2,000
70,000	45,000	50,000	50,000	25,000	20,000	20,000
140,000	115,000	100,000	92,000	25,000	40,000	48,000
210,000	185,000	150,000	134,000	25,000	60,000	76,000
280,000	255,000	200,000	176,000	25,000	80,000	104,000
350,000	325,000	250,000	218,000	25,000	100,000	132,000
420,000	395,000	300,000	260,000	25,000	120,000	160,000

According to these statistics Option 1 is preferable at every
level of profit above £70,000. The break-even is at a profit
level of £87,500.

17. DIANA COSMETICS Plc
Overall rate of absenteeism:

$$\frac{\text{Total days lost in month}}{\text{Total workdays in month}} \times 100$$

$$\frac{1905}{578 \times 20} \times 100 = \frac{190500}{11560} = 16.5\%$$

Under 21s rate of absenteeism:

$$\frac{1500}{200 \times 20} \times 100 = \frac{150000}{4000} = 37.5\%$$

Some more ideas on how to improve absenteeism?
(1) Good attenders to be included in a draw for Premium Savings
    Bonds or other special prizes.
(2) Collect information to determine where the problem lies.
    Which jobs? Which age groups? Long servers or recent
    recruits? Analyse data.
(3) Ensure there is a suitable induction programme so that new
    employees are given a full picture of the firm's operations
    and the roles they will be expected to play.
(4) Introduce flexible working hours and/or a shorter working
    week/day.
(5) Interview all absentees when they return. Discipline habitual
    offenders.
(6) Check recruitment and selection procedures.
(7) Accept a high rate of labour turnover for the workers. This
    could be seen as a type of job rotation between firms instead
    of jobs.

18. STRIKE NOW - PAY LATER
Consider the effect on this year's profits if (a) the sales
continue their downward trend and (b) if the workers achieve a
12% increase in pay. The effect of budgeting on the pay claim?

Graph - Figure 18.1
The argument runs thus. In the long run the price of any factor
of production, including labour, is determined by the forces of
demand and supply. The trade unions would appear to have defied
this economic law. But have they? Surely what happens is that
they force up the wages of their members but in doing this they
reduce the demand for workers generally in their firm or
industry. Inevitably, if wage rises are 'out of line' with price
increases for other factors, there will be a tendency for
capital-intensive methods of production to be favoured, and for
economies to be sought. Of course it is difficult to jettison
existing workforces but it is likely to be the unemployed who
face the barriers. The workforce will be run down and fewer new
jobs will be on offer.

How to cope with the shop stewards at Buchans
They represent an opportunity for the chief executive to short-
circuit the long chain of command. He can use them as a second -
and valuable - line of communication. To the extent that he can
convince them that his policies are logical and beneficial to
the workforce he can leave them to carry the message to their
workmates. He must also listen to them. Communication needs to be
a two-way process. They will no doubt have much to contribute.
What are their grievances? What attitudes exist on the shop-
floor? He has an opportunity to demonstrate to a small but
influential group of workers his genuine concern for the welfare
and prosperity of the workforce.

Of course it is easier to preach such doctrines than to
practise them. Yet what real alternatives are there to this
approach in a free society? Peregrine Worsthorne, reporting on
a visit to various Japanese companies, tells us of the different
attitude to decision-making which exists in that country:

> Critics of the Japanese factory system often describe it as
> unpleasantly reminiscent of military organisation, with the
> company modelled on the regiment, even down to the uniform
> and song. (The Japanese use the same word for foreman and
> corporal, incidentally.) Unquestionably there is also the
> same emphasis on hierarchy, discipline and group loyalty.
> Where the parallel seems to me to break down completely is in
> the way decisions are only taken after endless discussion
> involving everyone likely to be affected, the key word being
> consensus rather than command. Changes grow from the
> bottom upward, or at any rate are made to seem so by a
> management which describes its role as implementing ideas
> originating on the shop floor.
>
> (*Sunday Telegraph*, 28 March 1962)

19. THE BANK MANAGER - ROLE PLAY
With regard to the Squires' loan the bank manager will need to
make sure that the loan is not *ultra vires*. David Cox explains the
doctrine thus:

> All trading companies have an implied authority to borrow
> money and to give security, subject to any limitation imposed
> in the Memorandum of Association. One of the dangers of lending
> to a company is that the amount lent may exceed this limit.
> All lending beyond this amount would be known as *ultra vires* -
> beyond the powers of the company - and this phrase is used
> to describe any act not permitted by a company's Memorandum
> . . . However a lender, such as a bank, acting in good faith
> and unaware that a loan is outside the company's powers is
> protected by section 9 of the European Communities Act 1972,
> and would be able to recover the amount of the advance. This
> can place a bank in a difficult position because it very often
> has a copy of the Memorandum of Association in its files and
> therefore is deemed in law to be aware of any limitations
> on the company's borrowing. This problem . . . can be
> alleviated to some extent by requesting a certificate from

the company secretary stating that the proposed advance is within the powers of the company (and also within the powers of the directors, although this latter point is not so serious).

(Elements of Banking, John Murray 1979)

20. THE TWILIGHT VILLAGE

Since Dai mentioned the possibility of a takeover bid for the holiday camp one assumes it is possible to acquire the shares through purchases on a stock exchange. Dai Williams could therefore begin to buy shares in Snowdonia Holiday Camps but he would need to avoid a situation where his transactions pushed up the price of the shares unduly. Furthermore, while he would not want the directors of Snowdonia Holiday Camp to be aware of his intentions, under the Companies Act 1976 (Section 26) anyone acquiring 5% or more of the voting shares must notify the company in writing within a period of five days. This provision makes it difficult for Dai to 'warehouse' shares by distributing them among associates and colleagues while the takeover is proceeding. After Dai has acquired a substantial holding of voting shares - say, 30% - he will then make a formal offer to the remaining shareholders, no doubt offering to pay for their shares partly in cash and partly with shares of Tregaron. The problem is that they will probably appreciate by then the value of the land. If the cost of the takeover becomes prohibitive Dai may end up with a lot of shares in a holiday camp which are hard to dispose of.

21. THE FRENCH CONNECTION

Criticism of the marketing director's message

(1) Is it too long? Would readers lose interest before they got to the end of the passage?
(2) Does it lack visual impact? Pictures speak louder than words and in any case there should be some words in large print - some italics, sub-headings - in brief, there needs to be varying emphasis.
(3) 'Rather ordinary' Englishmen will not like being compared unfavourably with the 'knowing' French!

Questions which the Mooney board might ask

(1) Which of the companies is being taken over?
(2) What would be the effect of a break-down in the trading pattern between the two companies?
(3) How is M. Puisset to acquire a 40% share in the Mooney equity?
(4) What sort of language barriers are going to be encountered?
(5) What is known by the Mooney team about French commercial law?

22. JOINT CONSULTATION - GROUP ROLE PLAYING

How are decisions to be reached? By consensus? Or by voting?

23. MARSDEN MINI-RACERS
One of the risks faced by this business is fluctuating exchange
rates. David Cox explains the problem - and the remedy.

> Where payment for exporting goods is made in a foreign
> currency rather than in sterling, there is a danger that
> exchange rate fluctuations occurring between the date of
> shipment and the date of payment may reduce the exporter's
> profit or even turn the transaction into a loss. This problem
> can be overcome by the trader entering into a forward
> foreign exchange contract with his bank. The essence of such
> a contract is that the bank agrees to buy the foreign currency
> from the exporter at the date of payment at a certain fixed
> exchange rate; thus whatever happens to exchange rates in
> the interim, he always knows how much he will receive. The
> risk of changes in the exchange rates can thus be removed
> from the businessman's calculations, while the bank covers
> its own position by matching deals.
>
> (*Elements of Banking,* John Murray, 1979)

24. HIRSCHEL INDUSTRIES
One of the most popular methods of raising funds for companies is
by means of a rights issue. A Provisional Allotment Letter is
sent to the shareholders offering them the new shares on
favourable terms *pro rata* with their existing holdings. Merits?

From the company's point of view
(1) Since the new shares are offered at a favourable price the
    company can be sure of obtaining the funds.
(2) If the price offered is over-generous it is only the existing
    shareholders who are benefiting.
(3) It is likely to prove acceptable to shareholders if they see
    their money being put to good use - so long as the amounts
    are not too large.

From the shareholder's point of view
(1) He has a chance to acquire a bigger stake in a company he
    sees as being successful.
(2) He can sell the rights to the shares if he does not want to
    take advantage of the offer.
(3) He can sell sufficient of the rights to put him in funds to
    take up the remainder if he is short of funds but would like
    to buy as many shares as he can.

Pre-emption rights
Under Section 17 of the Companies Act 1980 a company proposing
to issue equity shares or convertible debentures for cash must
first offer them to existing shareholders in proportion to
their existing holdings. Section 18 of the Act allows these
pre-emption rights to be varied so long as the exclusions or
modifications are covered in the Articles of Association or by
Special Resolution.

Select Bibliography

For background reading and further study in specific areas.

DECISION-MAKING

H. I. Ansoff (ed.), *Business Strategy* (Penguin, 1969).
J. Clifford, *Decision Making in Organisations* (Longman, 1976).
A. Koutsoyiannis, *Non-Price Decisions: The Firm in a Modern Context* (Macmillan, 1982).
C. J. Margison, *Managerial Problem-solving* (McGraw-Hill, 1974).
J. R. Morrison, D. B. Hertz and L. V. Gerstner Jr, *Decision-Making: The Chief Executive's Challenge* (British Institute of Management, 1972).

MANAGEMENT

J. L. Burbridge, *The Principles of Production Control,* 4th edn (Macdonald & Evans, 1978).
J. C. Denyer, *Industrial Administration,* 3rd edn (Macdonald & Evans, 1979).
D. Foster, *The Management Quadrille* (Pitman, 1980).
J. Hargreaves, *Good Communications: What Every Manager Should Need to Know* (Associated Business Programmes, 1977).
T. Kempner (ed.). *A Handbook of Management A-Z,* 3rd edn (Penguin, 1980).
C. Woodcock (ed.), *The Guardian Guide to Running Small Businesses,* 2nd edn (Kogan Page, 1981).

PERSONNEL

P. Armstrong and C. Dawson, *People in Organisations* (ELMS, 1981).
R. Bennett, *Managing Personnel and Performance: An Alternative Approach* (Business Books, 1981).
D. Biddle and R. Evenden, *Human Aspects of Management* (Institute of Personnel Management, 1980).
A. Evans, *What Next at Work? A New Challenge for Managers* (Institute of Personnel Management, 1979).
I. MacKay, *A Guide to Asking Questions* (British Association for Commercial and Industrial Education, 1980).
P. Ribbeaux and S. E. Poppleton, *Psychology and Work: An Introduction* (Macmillan, 1978).

FINANCE
J. Chilver, *Investment: A Student-Centred Approach* (Macmillan, 1982).
D. Cox, *Elements of Banking* (John Murray, 1979).
F. W. Paish and R. J. Bristow, *Business Finance*, 5th edn (Pitman, 1978).
D. Parkinson, *Finance* (Blandford Press, 1979).

ACCOUNTING
R. J. Bull, *Accounting in Business*, 4th edn (Butterworth, 1980).
G. A. Lee, *Modern Financial Accounting*, 3rd edn (Nelson, 1981).
T. Lucey, *Management Information Systems* (DP Publications, 1980).
N. Thomson, *Management Accounting* (Heinemann, 1978).
P. Wood, *Business Accounting*: Vol. 2, 3rd edn (Longman, 1980).

STATISTICS
C. Evans, *The Making of the Micro: A History of the Computer* (Victor Gollancz, 1981).
J. E. Freund and F. J. Williams, *Elementary Business Statistics: The Modern Approach*, 3rd edn (Prentice-Hall, 1977).
C. S. Greensted, A. K. S. Jardine and J. D. Macfarlane, *Essentials of Statistics in Marketing*, 2nd edn (Heinemann on behalf of the Institute of Marketing and the CAM Foundation, 1978).
D. F. Groebner and P. W. Shannon, *Business Statistics: A Decision-Making Approach*, (Charles E. Merrill, 1981).
T. H. Wonnacott and R. J. Wonnacott, *Introductory Statistics for Business and Economics*, 2nd edn (John Wiley, 1977).

MARKETING
M. J. Baker, *Marketing: An Introductory Text*, 3rd edn (Macmillan, 1979).
B. Chiplin and B. Sturgess, *Economics of Advertising*, 2nd edn (Holt, Rinehart & Winston with the Advertising Association, 1981).
D. Enet, *Exporting for Small and Medium Sized Firms* (Business Books, 1977).
J. M. Livingstone, *International Marketing Management* (Macmillan, 1976).

ORGANISATIONS
J. M. Baddeley, *Understanding Industry* (Butterworth in association with the Industrial Society, 1980).
J. G. Capey and N. R. Carr, *People and Work Organizations* (Holt, Rinehart & Winston, 1982).
C. B. Handy, *Understanding Organizations*, 2nd edn (Penguin, 1981).
J. Harvey, *The Organisation in its Environment* (Macmillan, 1980).
E. F. Huse and J. L. Bowditch, *Behaviour in Organisations: A Systems Approach to Managing*, 2nd edn (Addison-Wesley, 1977).
L. Tivey, *The Politics of the Firm* (Martin Robertson, 1978).

INDUSTRIAL ECONOMICS

G. C. Allen *et al.*, *Mergers, Take-overs and the Structures of Industry* (Institute of Economic Affairs, 1973).

K. Heidensohn and N. Robinson, *Business Behaviour: An Economic Approach* (Philip Allan, 1974).

R. W. Moon, *Business Mergers and Take-over Bids*, 5th edn (Gee & Co., 1976).

W. Duncan Reekie, *Industry Prices and Markets* (Philip Allan, 1979).

INDUSTRIAL RELATIONS

Central Office of Information, *Trade Unions*, Reference Pamphlet 128 (HMSO, 1975).

H. A. Clegg, *The System of Industrial Relations in Great Britain* (Blackwell, 1978).

T. L. Johnson, *Introduction to Industrial Relations* (Business Books, 1981).

M. Moran, *The Politics of Industrial Relations* (Macmillan, 1977).

LAW

E. R. Hardy Ivamy, *Principles of the Law of Partnership*, 11th edn (Butterworth, 1981).

S. B. Marsh and J. Soulsby, *Business Law*, 2nd edn (McGraw-Hill, 1981).

M. C. Oliver, *Company Law*, 8th edn (Macdonald & Evans, 1981).

M. Whincup, *Modern Employment Law*, 3rd edn (Heinemann, 1980).